George Cooper was born in  Lyminster Farm, near Crewkerne. Educated at Crewkerne S_____ _____ _____, Crewkerne Grammar School and Wadhan Comprehensive School; he attended St.Paul's College, Cheltenham between 1974 and 1978, where he gained a B. Ed Honours degree through Bristol University. He was a well respected, innovative and popular Head of History, Head of Year, and a PE teacher working in state Schools in Crewkerne and at Millfield Preparatory School. At present, he works at the thriving Richard Huish 6th Form College in Taunton, where his main role is Director of Rugby.

He is well known in Somerset sporting circles. A Rugby Football Senior Coach, he is a life member of Crewkerne Rugby Club where he was both captain and senior coach in the 1970s and 1980s. He then coached Bridgewater & Albion RFC for six years from 1989-1995, winning the Somerset Cup three times in a row and gaining two promotions. For the past five years he has been Head Coach at Ivel Barbarians RFC in Yeovil. A keen cricketer, George opens the batting for the 2nd XI, at North Perrott C.C. whose magnificent ground enjoys a national reputation.

Married to Wendy, who played hockey and tennis for Somerset, their three children follow on in their parents sporting footsteps. Katherine (19) and Sarah (18) competed at national level in Gymnastics. They both play hockey for Somerset, the Taunton Vale and Cardiff University 1st XI's. Gareth (17) attends Kingswood School, Bath, the spiritual home of the Cooper family since 1850. He is a keen cricketer and rugby player, representing the school 1st XV and 1st XI as well as North Perrott Cricket Club.

AND HITLER STOPPED PLAY

**Cricket and War
at Lyminster House
West Sussex (1931-1946)**

George Cooper

George Cooper (signature)

And Hitler Stopped Play

Cricket and War at Lyminster House West Sussex (1931-1946)

Vanguard Press

VANGUARD PAPERBACK

© Copyright 2001
George R Cooper

The right of George Cooper to be identified as author of this work has been asserted by him in accordance with the Copyright, Designs and Patents Act 1988

All Rights Reserved

No reproduction, copy or transmission of this publication may be made without written permission.
No paragraph of this publication may be reproduced, copied or transmitted save with the written permission or in accordance
with the provisions of the Copyright Act 1956 (as amended).

Any person who does any unauthorised act in relation to this publication may be liable to criminal prosecution and civil claims for damage.

A CIP catalogue record for this title is available from the British Library
ISBN 1 903489 08 3

Vanguard Press is an imprint of
Pegasus Elliot MacKenzie Publishers
www.pegasuspublishers.com

First Published in 2001

Vanguard Press
Sheraton House Castle Park
Cambridge England

Printed & Bound in Great Britain

Dedication

To Major Charles Cecil Cooper, my grandfather.

Finchley, North London 1893-20
Manangatang, The mallee, Northern Victoria 1920-31
Lyminster Farm, West Sussex 1931-46
Wayford manor Farm, Crewkerne 1946-54
Lyminster Farm, Woolminstone, Crewkerne 1954-61
Combe St. Nicholas, Nr. Chard 1961-73

To Linda, Polly, Richard and Margaret Cooper, who joined him on his journey.

'To love and bear; to hope till hope creates from its own wreck the thing it contemplates.'

Prometheus Unbound IV

P B.Shelley (1792-1822)

ACKNOWLEDGEMENTS

Steve Green
Francis Pagan
Rosemary Anne Sisson
Lady Hazel Woodruff
John Leslie, Refreshers C.C.
Lady Jennifer Williams
Johnnie Johnson, Slinfold
Sir Michael Woodruff
Lord Ravensdale
Wendy, Katherine, Sarah and Gareth Cooper
Margaret Cooper
Trevor Steer
Alan Campbell-Johnson
Mrs Fay Campbell-Johnson
Maj. Gen. Errol Lonsdale
Christopher Alderson
Mrs. Lonsdale
Daphne Byrne
West Sussex County Council
Harry Butler
Mr. Pallas
The BBC
Mr. Gibb
Sir Ralph Kilner Brown
Mr.and Mrs Evans, Lyminster
Meg Budd
The Symes-Thompson family
Andrew Budd
Emma Rogers
John Lewis, Kingswood School Old Boys Association
Eunie "Auntie Mac" Gilbert

Polly Hankinson
Diana Brown
Dr. Philippa Dove
Catherine Maddock
Judy Falla
Judith Buckland
John Flood
Maj. Gen. Ronnie Buckland
Brigadier G.R. Flood
Frances Farrah-Brown
Yeoma Woolley
Judith Gauntlett
The Craxton Family
Mary Gale
George Carmen
Helen Robinson
Rev. Slegg, Lyminster
Hazel Crozier, R.A.F. Museum, Hendon
Julie Jones
J.B. Weatherill (Lepine family research)
Jill Craig
Bill Beere, Arundel Chamber of Commerce
Sir Richard Doll
Tim McCurry, West Sussex Records Office
Sir John Osborne
E.W.Swanton
Rebecca Fordell, Littlehampton Museum
Littlehampton Town Council
The Cricketer magazine
The Daily Telegraph
Rosemary Foot [nee Cooper]
Maj. Gen. Erroll Lonsdale
Clive Ellis, Airport Archive, Shoreham Airport
Emma Rogers, Littlehampton Gazette
Somerset County Cricket Club Museum
Sheila Ruffle, Librarian, The North London Collegiate School for Girls

Contents

Introduction		1
Chapter One :	The Cooper family	8
Chapter Two :	The Browns arrive at Lyminster House, West Sussex	19
Chapter Three :	Australian drought, snakes and sandstorms	28
Chapter Four :	Great Aunt Vi and Uncle Cecil Brown	43
Chapter Five :	"The solemn Trifler with his boasted skill."	50
Chapter Six :	1932 - "Ale and home-made apple pie."	60
Chapter Seven :	1933 - "For King and Country."	68
Chapter Eight :	1934 - "Fairy godparents wanted!"	79
Chapter Nine :	1934 - "Haven't declared yet......they have!"	84
Chapter Ten :	1935 Spectators - the people of Lyminster	87
Chapter Eleven :	Edmund Symes-Thompson - cavalier cricketer	102
Chapter Twelve :	1936 - Berlin Olympics, Spanish Civil War, the Triflers' first tour to Scotland.	110
Chapter Thirteen :	1936 - A Lyminster House Christmas.	119
Chapter Fourteen :	1937 - The Stanfords of Slinfold C. C. and Bates the Policeman.	123
Chapter Fifteen :	1938 - "Peace in our time."	131
Chapter Sixteen :	1939-"I have just spoken on the phone to the Prime Minister...."	147
Chapter Seventeen :	1940 - "The Battle of Britain."	163

Chapter Eighteen:	1941-"Linda......unfinished business!"	183
Chapter Nineteen :	1942 - "The fall of Singapore and the Dieppe raid."	186
Chapter Twenty :	1943 - "The beginning of the end."	196
Chapter Twenty One :	1944 - D Day, June 6th.	202
Chapter Twenty Two :	1945 - VE Day and the move from Lyminster	214
Chapter Twenty Three :	Wayford Manor Farm, Crewkeme.	226
Chapter Twenty Four :	The Triflers' Cricket Club. 1932-1940.	237

Introduction

The 1930's! Chamberlain's waving handkerchief, Hitler storming out of the 1936 Berlin Olympics, Country House cricket matches – three enduring images of the decade. The all have a direct connection with our story at Lyminster House, West Sussex. Pause a moment and take a peek into life in my Great Uncle Cecil and Aunt Vi Brown's Georgian house in the village of Lyminster. Peer over the ha-ha wall, which separated the expansive lawns from their magnificent cricket ground. One can almost hear the strains of Pomp and Circumstance echoing forth, forget any stereotypical picture of traditional England though. The Browns and their close relatives the Coopers were decades ahead of their contemporaries in terms of the emancipation of women. Achieving their goals through scholarships, not silver spoons, they would balked at today's political correctness and positive discrimination. The Coopers and Browns pertained to be Socialists and Liberals, but were also traditionally conservative in a Burkean sense. They were the epitome of a "Miss Marple" England, but without the murder! Committed Methodists, but also non-conformists in the very widest sense of the word, my ancestors sincerely believed in "Education! Education! Education!" This is in contrast to the unfulfilled Election winning slogan of 1997.

This chronicle of the two families is a contrasting tale. The Browns were idealists without! Great Uncle Cecil and

Great Aunt Vi Brown were wealthy, but benevolent, not out of any great sense of guilt, but because they genuinely wanted to do good deeds with their money. My Cooper grandparents, father Richard and his sister Polly were rescued from their drought stricken Australian farm in one such deed. My Grandfather's experiences in both wars are revisited, along with his great farming struggle in Australia. He was one of Kitchener's original 250 volunteers in August 1914. The growing crisis in Europe is charted alongside the great cricket battles against famous Sussex clubs on the Brown's beautiful Lyminster ground. Cricket dominates our story, but this is far from a straightforward cricket book. It is uncanny how famous events and people of the 30s had a connection in some way or another with the cricket at Lyminster House. The build-up to war has special significance as another Great Aunt in the Cooper clan was married to a member of Chamberlain's Cabinet.

This book is really the result of a lifelong curiosity about what happened at Lyminster, West Sussex all those years ago. We 40 something's are really the last gossamer thread which links Old England to New England. The well mannered, received pronunciation English with a measured sense of self-deprecation is the world in which I grew up. All these characteristics were inherent in the Cooper family. My generation may have rebelled against the more constraining aspects of Old England, but the children of the 1970 Isle of Wight Pop Festival soon adapted to short hair, suit and tie. The massive irony is that the 21st Century's new role models who ooze self-indulgence and mean-spirited egocentricity, were never meant to be the products of an England renowned for its politeness and reflective dignity. "Old England" is, perhaps, the only group of people left who are not protected by the "Equal Opportunities Commission".

Anything or anybody tainted with that label is mocked and met with almost vitriolic prejudice. The sense of fair play, modesty and a willingness to be absolutely straight as the straightest of bats in dealing with all things to do with mankind, are the inherent qualities of "Old England". Good manners were valued. Rural villages were bubbling communities where everybody knew each other. Crime was non-existent. Ordinary folk seemed far happier in a less materialistic world.

The village cricket ground is perhaps the last bastion of traditional village life. The shop, Post Office, bank and pub being sacrificed to the false idol of short term profitability. We then call this part of the process "modernisation"! For what purpose? What will we become? It will soon be possible to live in a village and never speak to another soul. In time, village cricket grounds may suffer the same fate as that of other amenities. They could be turned into open air museums, specialist guides trying in vain to explain to tourists how the game was once played.

The seeds of this book started on my Grandfather's knee, listening to stories about him riding his motorbike through the water-filled shell holes of Ypres. The liberal use of the quaint adjective "bally" adding atmospheric authenticity to the experience. The re-enactment included special effects. Being thrown into the air simulated hitting the frozen ruts of Flanders mud and was rather hair raising at times.

From an early age, we would select cricket teams. Grandpa Cooper would pick the heroes of the first three decades of the 20th Century. Names like Palairet, Rangi and Hobbs passed into my subconscious through a form of cricketing osmosis. I would select the Somerset side with Bill Alley always first name down. A game of "Owzat" would ensue. Two multi sided metal barrels with runs and methods of dismissal etched on each face would be rolled according to the rules. Its funny how simple things can give so much pleasure. Tales of the cricket at Lyminster in the 1930s fascinated me. The art of story telling is almost lost today.

As I passed into my teenage years, I always kept an immaculately cut and rolled wicket in the garden. Cricket nets completed a good home made practice facility. Groups of boarders from Crewkerne School would cycle out to Lyminster Farm and they filled the nets through long summer days of the early 70s.

My Grandfather told me of two cricket teams run by the Browns and Coopers in the 1930s; the striped blazered Lyminster Triflers formed from a group of Old Boys from Westminster School and the more local Lyminster House village XI. Very often, the two teams cross fertilised, representing the egalitarian views of my family. Many Triflers went on to become eminent men, making a mark on the history of the last century.

Famous Test match players graced the Lyminster House cricket field. Some of the Triflers were never to return from the war as we follow them and my family through some of the great events and actions of 1939-1945 including the fall of Singapore, Dieppe, D.Day, Arnhem, the crossing of the Rhine and the work of the Allied Control Commission.

The Browns and Coopers arrived at Lyminster in 1931 from totally different backgrounds and set of circumstances. They shared a love of family, of England and of cricket, a game which reflected the ideals in which they dearly believed. Cricket has had a long tradition in my family, it is ingrained in our genes. It represents a continuity which spans most of this century. Even if the old class system got in the way at times, the English sense of fair play and playing to the rules used to be exemplified by the phrase, "Its not cricket". Unfortunately, these values are no longer apparent in either the English or the game of cricket. Today, players need the quick fix of playing in Leagues in order to find inspiration, the idea of playing the game for the love of it would not register in the not so brave new world of cricket. Cricketers now accept cheating as a way of life. Appealing for catches which hit the ground, abusing the opposition and justifying this by stating that everybody does it, and of course, its just a natural progression of competitiveness. Worst of all, is the appalling betting and match fixing scandals which have left a rancid taste in the mouth of the game across the World. There was always a feeling in England of belonging to something associated with the greater good. Thankfully, the 2001 Australian cricket's team visit to Gallipoli represents a long awaited desire to understand the present through revisiting the sacrifices of forefathers. In contrast, Blair's dreadfully labelled "Cool Britannia" smugly sneers at its legacy.

The manner in which the game was played used to be as important as the actual result itself, encompassing a range of visual contrasts on the field of play. The cover drive, especially if played 'on the up', a work of art, sculptured only by batsmen with a sense of timing, waiting for the ball to arrive on the blade and caressing it to the boundary along a closely cropped carpet of grass. In fact it was the late Lord Cowdrey, ex aptain of Kent and the M.C.C. who stated that this one shot alone reflects Englishness and our culture more than any other single aspect of sport. Watching the flight of a spin bowler compares with the throwing of clay on a potter's wheel, the rhythm of skilled hands at work, patience being the virtue in order to trap the batsmen into a false shot. A spider's web of deceit. The quicker ball pushed through on a flatter trajectory, followed by the flighted delivery thrown high into the air, taking an eternity to reach the batsmen, only to dip quickly at the end of its' 20 yard journey. The anxious batsmen tempted to hit out indiscriminately in a rush of blood to the head, never quite being to the pitch of the ball. Perhaps the greatest feat of all is the leg side stumping, the wicket-keeper taking the ball and removing bails simultaneously in a cloud of dust as the batsmen desperately seeks to regain his ground; the drama heightened by a volcanic appeal which echoes around both ground and church lane.

In 1931 the Browns arrived in Lyminster and turned a simple Sussex field into a cricket ground the equal of anywhere in pre-war England. Cricket at Lyminster House epitomised the aesthetic appeal of the game. It was a golden era of the game played in its heyday; ivory flannelled players glowing on striped shades of emerald grass. Members of the Lyminster teams walked when they snicked the ball and only viewed sledging as a winter occupation on the Sussex Downs. They certainly didn't feel the need to keep up a constant cackle, much beloved of modern players, who think that shouting out the bowlers name before every ball bowled, somehow provides a modern mode of motivation. The bowler feels cosseted and his ego massaged. If bowlers produce a delivery wide of the off stump which is promptly left by the batsman, the slips break into a frenzy of applause. Village clubs copy what they see on the television, feeling that they themselves, have become modernised in the process.

Hitler's invasion of Poland stopped play at Lyminster in September, 1939. Spent cartridges from dog fights rained down on the outfield within a year, as our pilots chased Goering's Luftwaffe in the Sussex skies. Elgar verses Wagner. Nimrod fighting the Ride of the Valkyries. Vapour trails weaving intricate patterns, painting the paths of hunter and hunted. If we could talk to the ghosts who might walk the site of the old ha-ah wall, which separated the outfield from the Lyminster House gardens, what would they have to say? Luckily, four of the original Lyminster Triflers XI still survive to tell the tale. More than anything else though, this is my family's story, for the Coopers lived opposite the Browns in Church Lane, Lyminster. A story which weaves cricket, war and a whole range of famous names, who in one way or another had a unique connection with Lyminster House, West Sussex.

Chapter 1

The Cooper family

Before the 1st World War, all my grandfather's sisters were educated to a high level, they came from a pretty basic Victorian middle class background, nothing too pretentious, just a couple of servants and elocution lessons for all. These "blue stockings" played sport to a high level at a time when it was thought that a woman would turn into a man if she indulged in athletic activity! Sport was predominant in other branches of the family As recently as May, 2000, great uncle Cecil Brown's niece Audrey, recounted on BBC Radio 4's Woman's Hour her experiences at the Hitler Olympics at Berlin in 1936 She won a silver medal in the sprint relay. Her brother Godfrey went one better, winning gold and silver. Unfortunately, brother Ralph had been selected for the Olympics, but had to withdraw through injury. Audrey was one of only 28 women in the British Olympic team of 1936. Great aunt Vi Brown, nee Cooper, the sister of my grandfather, won one of the first 1st Class Honours degrees from Girton College, Cambridge and a hockey blue. They were pioneers, a incredibly tiny minority in England who paved the way for today's women on the sports fields of the world.

Of my fathers' 21 first cousins, he was the only male Cooper to produce a male! I was the last Cooper. This always made me a favourite with my exceedingly kind, but to a young boy, slightly eccentric and ageing great aunts. Unbeknown to me at the time, they would become the inspiration behind the writing of this book My great aunt Brenda was a favourite of all the nephews and nieces in the family. She kept vast amounts of family memorabilia and when she died, left her money to all the offspring of her brothers and sisters In character, she was Joyce Grenfall in overdrive mode. Ironically, she was the poorest of all her family peers. Brenda kept the following entry in her family log book concerning my father Richard Cooper,

From the schoolboy days of Richard when I was proud to back his rugger on the playing fields of Kingswood School, Bath to his wedding in that wonderful setting in Perthshire amongst an almost James Barrie atmosphere and later during a convalescence he took at Rock Cottage, Worthing with me after an operation at St Barts; and the sincere interest he showed in my late marriage to a very timid little gentleman, my heart always went out to Richard. I loved his children and his wife Margaret and I still do. Georgie, his son, is the sole male Cooper descendant and in him the qualities of his Dad and granddad are something to be proud of to hand on to posterity. Richard was one of those who died in that spell of bereavement which so tragically hit our family in the 60s.

The Coopers, 1906
Back: Voilet, Stephanie, Dorothy, Cecil

Front: Harold Woodruff, Margaret, Mary,
Basil, Charles, Brenda, Elsie.

What were these qualities? Daphne Byrne remembers my grandfather as, "A fine upstanding Englishman, as they say and the most impressive of all the family." Both he and my father were beautifully spoken gentlemen with perfect manners who treated others with dignity. Never afraid to sneak out publicly they always showed great courage in search of the truth.

The Coopers were a formidable Methodist family with one Huguenot branch going back to their escape from Flanders just two weeks before the St. Bartholomew's Day Massacre in 1572. There was a price on our heads even in those days! Jehan de Lespine left La Gorgue in August of that fateful year, rowing across the English Channel under the cover of darkness with seven other Protestant refugees of those bloody times. Legend has it that the actual name Lespine, or "the point", derives from the Crusades. King St. Louis of France recieved the "Crown of Thorns" from Saladin, and entrusted it to one of his knights, a Norman, who became thereby "le Chevalier de L'Epine" - the "Knight of the Thorn".

A few days after Jehan's escape, over 25,000 men, women and children were slaughtered on the orders of the Catholic Charles IX and his mother Catherine de Medici. Jehan must have been singled out by the Catholic authorities. My Huguenot ancestors were asylum seekers long before the present Balkan crisis, escaping from a religious form of ethnic cleansing. Sanctuary was given at Canterbury Cathedral, where the Huguenots were given their own chapel. Before too much vicarious sympathy is extended towards the Huguenots, it is worth remembering that they would have done the same to the Catholics given half a chance. Indeed, it was Oliver Cromwell who was to terrorise the Irish Catholics of Wexford and Drogheda within the next hundred years. The Huguenot influence has always lived on in our family, enabling us to stand up for what is right. As a young boy, I made sure that I only swore as many times as I was of chronological age. Therefore, by the age of 11, I had sworn only 11 times. Many years later in my teaching career, nine-year-olds had the ability to swear 11 times in one sentence. Such is the price of progress and the entitlement age! I think we Coopers are more than comfortable holding the opposite view or being in a minority of one. The silk-weaving Lepines (the name had been shortened in the seventeenth century) set up home in London. It was here where their descendants met the Coopers in early Victorian times.

My extended family were still remarkably closely linked in the 1950s and 1960s. Many of them were rich or eminent people in the fields of business, medicine or politics. My immediate family were what is affectionately termed as the 'poor relations'. On my extended family tree, there are four MPs; one Cabinet Minister; two PPCs who stood but were never elected; four Sirs; ten Methodist Ministers; five JPs and a famous surgeon; and some exceedingly rich businessmen.

Grandpa Cooper was the third youngest of nine Cooper children brought up in Seymour Road, Finchley, opposite the Ballards Road Methodist Church. The eldest Cooper, Margaret, married Harold Woodruff, later Professor of Veterinary Pathology and Director of the Veterinary Institute in the University of Melbourne. She died of septicaemia in 1917; her children, Michael and Philip, were aged six and three at the time. In 1925, they were page-boys at my grandfather's marriage to Linda Metherall in Sea Lake, Victoria. Both Woodruff boys followed medical careers. Michael, a famous surgeon who would perform Britain's first kidney transplant, was knighted at Holyrood Palace in 1969. Philip Woodruff became Director of Public Health in South Australia. Violet Cooper was the second eldest and married Cecil Brown, the son of a Methodist Missionary on June 1st, 1910. We will learn more about the Browns, for this story is centred around them.

Front left: Athol (Australian Army), Cecil (An "Old Contemptible") and Dr. Basil Cooper.

1918 Soldier, Soldier, Doctor.

The next, Dorothy Cooper, married Leslie Burgin, who lived opposite the Coopers in Seymour Road. He later became Minister of Transport in 1936 and subsequently the first 'Minister of Supply' in Neville Chamberlain's ill-fated 1939 wartime government. Stephen Cooper died whilst a young baby. Stephanie married Frank Woodruff, a name at Lloyd's of London and brother of Harold. The next, Atholl, became an Australian MP and was my grandfather's original farming partner in Australia; he married an Australian, Dorothy Holmes.

Brenda Cooper was the youngest girl and had to take on the role of 'maiden aunt', looking after her ageing mother Mary in Finchley until they were both evacuated to Limpley Stoke near Bath in 1941, when Brenda's firm, the Abbey Manor Building Society, relocated there during the Blitz. She later married at the age of 59! Elsie Cooper married Aubrey Holmes in Australia, brother of Dorothy Holmes. The youngest Cooper, Basil, became a doctor: he trained at St Bartholomew's Hospital, London and played in five Hospitals Rugby Cup Finals in the early 1920s. He married a nurse, Sally Court, which led some of the family to rather cruelly say, 'Sally caught Basil'.

Stephen Fry, playing a WW1 General in Richard Curtis and Ben Elton's classic comedy series, famously exclaimed in one episode that

The trouble with women, Blackadder, is that they simply just don't know the value of a good forward defensive shot!

This would not have applied to the Cooper girls! My great-grandfather, Charles Cooper, had encouraged all his five girls to play sport to a high level and go to university. Not the norm for Edwardian England around the turn of the century! Equality of opportunity is not such a new phenomenon. In June 1913, Mrs Bryant, Headmistress of the famous North London Collegiate School for Girls wrote the following letter to Charles Cooper, my great grandfather:

The North London Collegiate School for Girls

12th June 1913

Dear Mr Cooper,

I am sorry for the time for Brenda to leave, but I did understand that it would be soon. I think she has been very happy, and as regards to the position she has taken here, she will leave the same delightful impression behind her as all the other Coopers have done.

Yours sincerely,
Sophie Bryant

Margaret, Vi, Stephanie, Dorothy, Elsie and Brenda Cooper had graced the most famous girls school in England. Steph and Elsie went to Reading University, the former playing for the 1st XI hockey team and Vi went on to Cambridge. Vi broke the Girton College hockey goal-scoring record, won a Blue, and became a single figure handicap golfer. She also played cricket for Girton College, which had access to a coach and regular fixtures against other Colleges such as Newnham. On May 26th, 1907, Vi Cooper and Muriel Gibbon put on 55 runs for the eighth wicket in 35 minutes. Vi made 35 of these and the partnership resulted in Girton's first win over their opponents for six years. It was in 1910 that she married Cecil Brown, who would become a wealthy Underwriter at Lloyds of London. They had met at the Methodist Church in Finchley, the centre of social life for the Woodruff, Cooper, Burgin and Brown families in the Edwardian era.

All of my grandfather's sisters loved their sport, and as youngsters they played cricket in the park at Finchley, usually against their neighbours the Burgins, who would take on the Coopers until dusk brought an end to their games. As children, the Cooper sisters and brothers used to walk the six miles from their Finchley home to the Mecca of cricket, Lords, during that golden age of cricket before the outbreak of World War One. Violet's favourite player was Gilbert 'The Croucher' Jessop, whose son, the Revd G. L. O. Jessop would later grace their own ground at Lyminster whilst playing for Havant.

All three Cooper brothers went to Christ's College, Finchley, along with the Burgins. My grandfather was eminent in all of the school's sporting and military activities and just missed a scholarship to university, as a result of the male Cooper tendency toward sloppy use of English! Cricket, swimming and riding were his great loves. Before he started work as an Actuary in the City, the Commanding Officer of the Royal Horse Guards (The Blues) had wanted him to remain in the regiment which he had joined upon leaving school. Cricket dominated my grandfather's life and he saw W. G. Grace's last first class game at Lord's in 1904 when it snowed in the lunch hour! The MCC were playing South Africa, and Grace scored 27 before being brilliantly caught behind off Kotze, a lightning-quick bowler.

Spitfires and Mosquitoes

I was born in 1956, 23-4-56 to be precise! My upbringing was remotely rural in a close-knit family with a traditional set of values at Lyminster Farm, just outside the small hamlet of Woolminstone, two miles west of the town of Crewkerne. The soft rolling countryside of South Somerset was a glorious place to grow up. If my childhood was in any way misspent, then it was due to our garden becoming Twickenham and Wembley in winter and the County Cricket Ground, Taunton, in summer.

When not practising cricket, I was always attempting

to make model aeroplanes, World War Two vintage, out of Airfix kits. I say 'attempt' because I was blessed with five thumbs on each hand. However, I once succeeded rather well with a Spitfire. The propeller actually spun round when you flicked it. There had been a famous Spitfire airfield at Tangmere near Lyminster during the war. Douglas Bader was stationed there before he was shot down and captured. *Reach for the Sky* was the first film I ever saw on the television. My father and his sister Polly used to hare off around the Sussex countryside searching out crashed German planes.

I had far more trouble constructing the Mosquito. These were the aircraft which were based at Ford, even closer to my family's old home. A Mosquito crashed at Lyminster in 1943. It exploded just outside Aunt Vi and Uncle Cecil Brown's large Georgian house, where the ha-ha met the corner of the cricket field. The assembly of the Mosquito's fiddly cannons, housed on the nose-piece of that wonderful aircraft, was far too difficult to accomplish without covering my hands and the whole of the plane with that clear glue beloved of schoolboys of my era. It was the sort of glue which within ten seconds turned to that plastic string you squirt at each other, but only at Christmas. Unless you applied it quickly to the relevant parts, one's hands turned into a version of 'Cat's Cradle'. What is abundantly clear, though, is that cricket and the war left an indelible imprint on my childhood.

Our farm in Somerset was named after the Cooper and Brown families' time at Lyminster Farm in West Sussex. The milk from our herd of Guernseys was always stored in large churns, before daily collection by the milk lorry. If you could roll a full churn of milk across the milking parlour floor, then you were big enough to help the adults! The unpasteurised, thick creamy milk accompanied my cornflakes throughout childhood days. There were never any health scares involving food in my youth. We were immunised by being exposed to food in its natural state, not fed small supermarket packages of carefully wrapped cellophane, the product of the consumer society where food has undergone an ethnic cleansing of all its traditional characteristics! Each cow in the Cooper herd, founded in 1931, was rather quaintly named after an individual on our family tree. These herd names were retained until its sale in 1968.

Chapter 2

The Browns arrive at Lyminster House, West Sussex, 1931

St John's Wood, Lords and the Craxtons

In January 1931, CNB – Cecil Brown, Great-aunt Vi and their son Stephen made their move from 54, Circus Road, St John's Wood, just behind Lords cricket ground, to Lyminster House in Sussex, previously owned by the Duke of Norfolk. St John's Wood had been an ideal location for the Browns, close to Lloyd's and 'The City', in reasonable distance of Westminster School where son John was a pupil, and superbly placed for Lords. CNB had become exceedingly rich, but got his pleasure in life out of seeing the family benefit from his benevolence.

Around the corner from the Browns at St John's Wood lived the Craxton family. Anthony Craxton would also star on the cricket field at Lyminster in the 30s. In her 1953 autobiography, Aunt Vi said of Anthony that:

…his long musical fingers wrapped so far round a cricket ball that the venom of his spin was only palliated by the uncertainty of his length.

He later produced the first Outside Broadcasts of Test

Match Cricket in England for the BBC. Craxton was responsible for Brian Johnson and Peter West joining the commentary team. After becoming Head of Outside Sports Broadcasts, he produced the first Royal Documentary in 1967 and produced every Royal Wedding until 1973. I wonder what he would think of the 'Sky Sports'-dominated broadcasting world of today? His personal achievements seem a long way away from his childhood days when he and his brothers would sneak without paying into the Mound Stand at Lords through a gap in the fence! Anthony's brother recounted to me that a favourite prank of the Craxton boys was to empty out boxes of grass cuttings into a young Denis Compton's sports car!

August 9th 1940, Lyminster House. Note the ha-ha and overgrown cricket outfield. This picture was taken 9 days before the German raid on Poling and Ford.

"I'd rather watch the cricket!"
Polly Cooper (left) and Richard Cooper (right) in front of Lyminster House with Jill Burgin 1934.

When Uncle Cecil and Auntie Vi Brown bought Lyminster House and its 50-acre estate from the Duke of Norfolk in 1931, it was not an easy purchase as Ducal estates were notoriously awkward to deal with. Immediately they began to build their cricket ground in the environs of the house. Two teams were based there, the 'Triflers' Cricket Club', formed originally around a core of old boys from Westminster School, and the more rustic Lyminster House village XI. An old-fashioned English atmospheric scene of great charm and grace would prevail throughout the 30s and became very well known in the Sussex cricket scene.

The house and ground lay between Arundel, three miles to the north, and the coast at Littlehampton in the south. The seven-bedroomed, two-storied, late-Georgian house with gently-pitched slate roof and generous eaves was in urgent need of repair. It had been empty for two or three years and lagged behind the ordinary amenities of the day. Mains water ran past the gates but had not been connected, the water coming from several wells serviced by handpumps. There was no fitted bathroom and the kitchen was dark and gloomy. The thick stone passages were said by locals to clank with the 'sound of chains'. Sixty-seven years later I would be told of a very unpleasant ghost who caused more than a few problems over the years for Maj.-Gen. Ronnie and Judith Buckland, who have lived in the western wing of the house since 1977. The Browns later sold Lyminster to Air-Marshall Salmond, Head of the RAF. Their daughter Rosemary married Nicolas Mosley, son of the English Fascist, Sir Oswald. The Mosleys took over the house and lived there until the late 1960s.

At the end of Church Lane, Lyminster lived the Sisson family. Professor Sisson was a leading light in the field of Shakespearean literature. Polly Cooper remembers Rosemary and her sister Daphne skipping down the lane towards Lyminster Church, balloons billowing in the wind. A picture of happy innocence. Rosemary Sisson would later write *Elizabeth R*, *The Six Wives of Henry VIII* and *Upstairs, Downstairs*. In the 30s and 40s she always referred to Lyminster House as 'Brown's House'. The Sissons' house was later bought by Sir Roger Bannister.

In 1931, the Browns fell in love with the house and its environs. The property lay only 19 feet above sea level, yet seemed much higher. The charm and magic of the site was centred on the view to the north from the upstairs windows. A stretch of level lawn opened out between two wide-angled lines of lime trees which overlooked a large field, separated by a ha-ha. This large field is the centrepiece of our story. It became the field of cricketing dreams and, in post-war years, of warm and wonderful memories mixed with sadness at the thought of those players who never returned from the war. Modern legend has it that the round window on the front of the house was specifically added by one of the Dukes of Norfolk in the nineteenth century for his lover living at Lyminster House. If the light was on, he would come riding from Arundel Castle. An early form of mobile phone beacon? Unfortunately, photographic evidence from the 1930s shows that the round window never even existed then! What was certain is that over the years, the Dukes of Norfolk could walk from Sussex almost to London over land which they owned.

The cricket field

In 1931, the cricket field at Lyminster House was just a farmer's field, a bumpy area of land which sloped gently down to a conifer wood, in the middle of which the tops of old yew trees had been cut down to frame an exclusive picture of Arundel Castle, perched on a spur of the South Downs three miles to the north. The small corner of Sussex in our story is dominated by the magnificence of Arundel Castle's grand battlements, the ancestral home of the Duke of Norfolk, whose family have lived there since the sixteenth century. The building dominates the whole of the area. Although the castle is basically Victorian, there is a genuine medieval atmosphere about the whole building. During the 1939–45 war the US Army took over the east wing of the castle; they were joined by the Royal Observer Corps, who had a manned post in the keep, and the Home Guard, who occupied the south section during the Battle of Britain.

The three miles distance between the cricket field and Arundel lent enchantment to the castle, creating an illusion that Lyminster House was on the same level, the castle holding court over the soft green Sussex countryside which gently rolled its way to the coast at Littlehampton. Lyminster House itself was separated from the field by the magnificent ha-ha, thus elevating the lawns of the house over the level of field. The western boundary of the field was a double hedge of holly and macrocarpa, grown so tall that the sky was only just visible above it if you stood alongside it. Nineteen-year-old John Brown took one look at the field and in his mind's eye immediately transformed the field into the perfect cricket ground. He turned to his parents and exclaimed, 'If you don't buy this, I will never forgive you for having shown it to me.'

Plans were set to restore the house, stables, farm buildings and the cottage, Nyarrin, where my Cooper grandparents, Aunt Polly and father would take residence in Church Lane. The central focus of the whole property and estate would be the cricket ground. Money, it must be stressed, was no object to the Browns. In 1931, the Browns and Coopers started plans for the move into their new homes, the former in the large Lyminster House, and the latter in the cottage 200 yards away. It was called 'Nyarrin' after their old farm in Victoria,. My grandfather Cecil Cooper and his family, recent arrivals from Australia, initially lived in a rented cottage in nearby Rustington while he supervised the renovations at Lyminster. He began stocking the pedigree Guernsey herd and modernised the farm buildings. The Coopers had use of an old 12HP Morris car, mid-brown in colour, in which the temporary daily journey to Lyminster was made. Very early in that first year, young Polly and Richard Cooper started their careers as Sussex sea bathers, rather more bracing than the balmy dam waters of Manangatang, Northern Victoria, where they had learnt to swim. In each of the eight succeeding years, up to the start of the war, they always bathed at the end of April at Littlehampton, no matter how cold it was! The arrival of summer was celebrated in an annual shivering ceremony.

Young Polly Cooper remembers:

Across the lane was the high flint wall surrounding Auntie Vi and Uncle Cecil's Lyminster House, the walled fruit garden, the complex of other buildings including the Gardener's house, second Gardener's flat, Coach House, as well as the heated greenhouse, kitchen garden and shrubberies.

I always knew when my Dad was coming home from the farm office at Lyminster House because he would slam the big wooden double gate in the wall and the enormous contraption would reverberate with a loud crash. In the mornings I would watch Uncle Cecil Brown leave to catch the 8.15 train from Arundel station in order to get to Lloyd's, city-suited from Monday to Thursday, tweed-suited on a Friday.

All country houses have their story to tell. Lyminster House of the 1930s and 40s is an intriguing chronicle of a long-lost England. There are many anomalies surrounding Lyminster House in the 1930s. The Triflers' XI were basically a Public School old boys side and were a bastion of country house striped blazer cricket, but the Lyminster village team also played at the ground, and indeed they probably played more matches in total than the Triflers. The cross-fertilisation of the two teams was an amalgam which reflected the egalitarian views of Cecil and Vi Brown and the Triflers themselves. They were a group of old boys of Westminster School who themselves, in their individual ways, were idealists as well.

There were at least nine people in domestic service or employed in the gardens at Lyminster House and yet Aunt Vi Brown had joined the Labour Party during the 1926 General Strike. She would later drive her Daimler with a 'Vote Labour' sticker prominently displayed in the back window! For huge parties of Londoners from the deprived

Millwall area in the Isle of Dogs, Lyminster House was an annual holiday oasis. During the war, tea dances were held in Uncle Cecil's billiards room. All ranks from rapidly changing army units in the Lyminster area came to these dances; moving, mingling and mixing with WAAFs from RAF Ford and Radar Operators from Poling. Floating over the highly polished oak floor to the sound of Glenn Miller, Canadians, Americans, Scots and English troops escaped from the reality of war and very often found love in an English country house. Clearly, this is not just another stereotypical country house history amidst a class-ridden 'Old England'. The class system existed all right, but the Browns were forward-thinking and constantly challenged it.

Aunt Vi Brown loved to lock horns with the local aristocracy. After moving to Lyminster, visiting dignitaries would ask the boiler-suited gardener if the lady of the house was in: the reply was that they were addressing the selfsame person! A collection of formal calling cards were neatly tucked away in the pocket of Vi's overalls! The local aristocracy, who may have looked down on her in a social sense, found Vi's intellectual mind was too much to cope with and they labelled her as a 'bluestocking'. One such person was Evelyn Emmett from Amberley Castle, later in charge of the WRVS in the war. The establishment, though, stood no chance in a fair exchange of words. Vi was highly intelligent, a member of the Fabian Society and Cambridge-educated, winning, as you will recall, one of the first degrees (First Class) from Girton College.

Aunt Vi and Uncle Cecil Brown were benevolent in the great English nonconformist tradition of Cadbury and Rowntree, and indeed Vi became a committed Quaker in her latter years. The Browns were more concerned with how they spent their money rather than with how much of it they acquired. Today, they would be mocked and vilified. They were also nonconformists in the widest sense, not merely in a religious connotation. Aunt Vi Brown was a leader, a doer. She built communities. Opinionated? Yes! She would write long letters to the Archbishop of Canterbury questioning various aspects of Church of England dogma. There again, all the Coopers could be provocative and still are!!! Her idealism somewhat muddled? Sometimes. Champagne socialism did exist before 1997! The difference between her and the traditional landed aristocracy, though, is that anybody who had contact with the Browns benefited from the experience. Ask the people of Wayford, the village near Crewkerne where they moved to with my family in 1946. The Browns renovated every one of their farm workers' cottages, introducing all the modern post-war amenities. I am still stopped in the streets of my home town, Crewkerne, by folk who still talk warmly about 'the Browns'. Ask the poor from Millwall in the Isle Of Dogs who flocked to Lyminster House in the 1930s for summer days out. Ask the surviving farm workers who live around Lyminster in West Sussex. Vi Brown always encouraged individuals to better themselves through education. Ageing members of the Cooper and Brown family were looked after as they became infirm. Nobody benefited more from the Brown's actions, though, than my immediate family, the Coopers, as they were rescued from drought-induced starvation in Northern Victoria in 1931.

Chapter 3

Australian drought, snakes and sandstorms

The oldest 'Contemptible' of the Great War?

Grandpa Cooper had been one of Lord Kitchener's original 250 volunteers in 1914. It would be no surprise if he had been the first to sign up. He later volunteered for duty in the Second World War, although he was minus an eye by then. This probably made my Grandfather unique in British military history, the only member of Kitchener's first vintage crop to serve their country in the second campaign. In 1945 he ended the war as a Major in the Allied Control Commission in Hanover, overseeing food distribution to the starving refugees and displaced masses.

On August 8th, 1914, Grandpa Cooper had enlisted as a Despatch Rider with the Royal Engineers (Corporal in the 2nd Signal Coy of the 2nd Cavalry Division, 7th Hussars, number 28115), leaving Southampton on one of the first troop ships to France,

There was a regular supply of toffee, cake, the magazine *Punch*, and numerous other goodies out to the front from the Cooper family back in Finchley. As a motorcycle Despatch Rider, my grandfather was lent out to different Divisions for reconnaissance work. On August 26th, 1914 he worked with the 19th Hussars and was asked, 'Can you turn around and get away quickly if fired on?' He was sent ahead of the patrols, but saw no Germans in those fledgling days of World War One.

On September 3rd, the 19th Hussars were ordered up to the Marne, and Corporal Cooper stayed with them for the next few weeks. My grandfather's letters home to Finchley were full of self-deprecating humour and celebration of an adventure which would hopefully be the war to end to all wars. This front, if you excuse the pun, merely acted as a means to keep up spirits back home. The reality would be so different to the extract from following letter.

6th September, 1914

...We are not yet bound for the front so keep your hair on. Did I tell you about our German watching job last week? I was one of a patrol who spent the most of 4 days working about 7 miles from the base. The way I personally worked most of the time was by lying on my back in the shade and going to sleep.

The only blot on the landscape was having to shift my position under the tree every time the sun caught you up. I made several interesting acquaintances and practised my French on all and sundry...

Two days later, on the 8th, he took the Adjutant as a pillion passenger up to the Aisne. In early October, he accompanied the 2nd Cavalry Division towards and beyond Ypres via Cassel Kemmel, Messines, Gapard, Hollebeke and Klein Zillebeke. On October 11th, the Royal Horse Artillery galloped into action at Monts Des Cats, near Cassel. The monastery was shelled and Prince Max of Hesse was killed. He was a nephew of both the King and the Kaiser, rather a thought-provoking fact! Grandpa Cooper's 20th birthday on October 31st 1914 coincided with the climax of the first battle of Ypres.

First shell to hit Ypres Cathedral, 1914.

Ypres Cathedral, 1933. (Cecil Cooper) The Cathedral was still in the process of rebuilding.

Hill 60 Ypres, Linda Cooper 1933.

In March 1915, the 2nd Cavalry Division was standing by for a break through at Neuve Chapelle. At Reninghelst, south west of Ypres, the first chlorine gas was smelt: a faint green cloud was spotted by my grandfather as he was out of the line at the time. In mid-May he was carrying messages, mainly between Vlamertinghe and Hooge. Twenty-four trips were made on one particular day via Dead End (a canal north of Ypres), timed to miss the explosions of our 17 inch shells in Ypres. He was decorated with the Cross of St George of Russia for his actions and commissioned as a 2nd Lieutenant in the Royal East Kents, 'The Buffs' (1st Div., 12 Platoon). Unwittingly, he was perhaps the first officer to prevent his men from catching 'trench foot'. On December 19th, 1915, at Ypres, Cecil Cooper 'acquired' a store of gumboots and fitted up his platoon with the newly found footwear. None of his men suffered from this affliction of the feet. On Christmas Day, 1915, the rest of the whole of C Coy were immobilised! The 'Donkeys' running the war did not fully comprehend the significance of this discovery.

Grandpa also fought at the Battle of the Somme, where he was wounded at Combles. On the first day of the battle, he was recommended for the Military Cross for a wire-cutting exercise, but the officer in charge was killed before it could be sorted out. My grandfather ended the war in Salonica with a machine-gun company, guarding captured Turkish guns, four brass plates of which were unscrewed and kept as souvenirs – they now sit proudly in my mother's fireplace in Crewkerne, Somerset. Cecil Cooper never settled back to life in a suit in the City. The horror of the trenches spurred his dream to become a Soldier-Settler on 640 acres of farmland in Northern Victoria. This dream was to go sadly awry as dust-bowl drought replaced the muddy mire of the Flanders trenches.

Rescued by the Browns

Cecil Brown, 'CNB' to the family, had married my grandfather's sister, Violet Cooper, in 1910. The Browns, like the Coopers were an established Methodist family. There were many Methodist missionaries in Cecil Brown's family, men of God, but basically poor, spreading the Christian faith throughout the British Empire. My grandfather's war record was well respected in the family, and this, together with the desire to help the family were the principle reasons behind CNB's kindness towards his brother-in-law. In 1920, the Browns gave my grandfather £1,000 to make a start in Australia. They also paid for brother Basil Cooper's training at St Bartholomew's Hospital in London; he was the youngest brother of Vi and my grandfather.

On January 6th, 1920, my grandfather wrote to the

Browns from *RMS Grampion* on his way to Australia via Canada and reflected on the kindness shown to him by his sister and brother-in-law:

…I want you to know that any degree of success in life I may have, I owe, after allowing for Mother and Father's influence and bringing up. (I don't mean that is secondary to your material and not only material help.) Without the material help I have sufficient confidence to know that what strength I've derived from being a Cooper would above kept my head above water. I know that I'm going to make a show. I may never make a lot of money but, I know I'm going to be happy in Australia and afterwards in England.

Manangatang, Outback Victoria, Australia 1928.
Linda Cooper arrives with lunch for husband Cecil.

1990 The Mallee Roller. Polly Hankinson (nee Cooper) and Tim Langley (Grandson of Cecil Cooper's old family neighbour).

Manangatang, Victoria. Cecil Cooper's old farm, 1990.

Polly Hankinson (right) revisits Sea Lake War Memorial Hall where Cecil Cooper and Linda Metherall held their wedding reception on September 2nd, 1925.

The hardship of farming in semi-desert scrubland was an attraction in itself. Nothing could be as bad as the Flanders trenches and the challenge of turning such land into proper farmland was worth all the backbreaking work. He was joined at first by his brother Atholl, along with scores of other ex-soldiers from Britain. By the end of the decade, the *Argos*, the regional newspaper in Northern Victoria, was reporting:

The plight of the Mallee farmers is pitiable. On almost every occasion when showers have been falling in other parts of the State they have experienced the cruel disappointment of missing the falls altogether. In some parts of the north-west many farmers, influenced by the good outlook in the early autumn, have worked exceptionally hard to clear and cultivate additional land. They have prepared far more ground for sowing than in any previous season. The drift and storms have found little difficulty in dislodging the seed.

My grandfather sincerely believed that the rains would come, but they never did in sufficient quantity. His spirit remained undiminished and he wrote to his sister Brenda that the overall prospect was

...still good for our wheat if the rain is not too long delayed and the price will be higher than last year.

Two weeks later optimism still reigned:

We still have a chance of a small return without any more rain and a shower or two would make a difference.

At the end of 1929, he wrote to his sister Vi and stressed that

When the bumper years come, I for one am not forgetting the terrible drought years.

The bumper years never did come. In March 1930, my grandfather and grandmother, my father and his sister Polly were literally down to their last loaf of bread. Ten years after setting sail for the promised land, drought and dust storms resulted in the Browns bringing my grandfather back to England. It was not just benevolence which had provoked these actions, but a respect for Cecil Cooper's war record. CNB had been declared unfit for war service in 1914. Grandpa Cooper was now offered the job of running the Brown's newly purchased farm at Lyminster in Sussex and developing a pedigree Guernsey herd. Running the Lyminster House village XI was nearly as important!

The following letter outlines Uncle Cecil Brown's offer of a job at Lyminster House:

54, Circus Road
St John's Wood
NW8

14th August, 1930

My dear Cecil,
               I thought I would delay writing to you until I heard from Harold Woodruff (brother-in-law) which I have done this week and I now understand exactly how matters stand with you.

I have told Harold that I agree with all he has done and Vi has already written to you fairly fully so that it is not necessary for me to go into the financial details too closely.

I told Harold that a businessman's success is out of proportion to his efforts compared with other people's efforts (I didn't mean to infer that making money is the chief aim in life) so there must be a greater responsibility to use it properly and I can assure you and Linda that I feel it a privilege – it most emphatically is a pleasure to participate in your work in the only way I possibly can.

The only question I would like to ask is the amount of the first mortgage and the rate of interest?

Vi and John have gone on a P+O cruise (the Viceroy of India) to Norway and Iceland and from letters I have had they seem to be enjoying it – my dislike of the sea keeps me at home as I think I should enjoy my holidays on land better.

I hope John will go to Cambridge next year but what after that is in 'the lap of the gods'. His chief interests seem to be literature and cricket! I'm glad say he just managed to get his cricket 'pinks' at Westminster and I think he should do well next year. You are certainly blessed with your children and I only hope I will be able to see them before they are quite grown up – Harold says Mike and Pip (Woodruff) are almost men!

Well, the best of luck to you in your work and may you

have the bumper harvest you deserve.

Kind regards,
Cecil (Brown)

My grandfather replied with the following telegram in January 1931:

Passages booked on the 'SS Moreton Bay' from Melbourne. Stop. Exact time unknown. Stop. Will keep you informed. Stop.

Cecil Cooper.

It confirmed his decision to return to England. Cecil and Vi Brown rescued him, my grandmother, my father and his sister Polly from virtual starvation, paying for the journey home and providing a job, house and private schooling for the Coopers.

The fire and brimstone experienced by my grandpa on the Western Front was replaced by the scorched earth of the worst drought in the history of Victoria. The birdsong in the outback sounded even sweeter than that heard at the Armistice in November 1918, but it did not compensate for the fact that the farm had turned into a dust-bowl. Young Polly Cooper, my father's sister, was taught at an early age to say, 'Lovely thunder, lovely thunder!'

Correspondence had flowed freely between England and Australia in the 1920s, especially with the news of Grandpa's engagement to Gran Cooper. She was a third-generation Australian of Cornish and Scottish descent. Her family were farmers and she too worked the land, specialising in breaking in young horses, until she was badly thrown in 1927 whilst in the early stages of expecting her first child Polly. The resultant broken leg left her with a lifelong limp. That same year, Grandpa Cooper lost an eye after an accident chopping wood. A nurse wrongly moved him during hospital treatment and the damage became permanent. Grandpa's only comment after the accident was, 'The Coopers are apt to become a rather one-eyed lot!'

My father, Charles Richard Cooper, had been born out in Australia on March 12th, 1929, in Manangatang. Polly has always been renowned in the Cooper family for her long-term memory: although only two and three quarters when her brother was born, she recounts that

> I can remember that going into the hospital and sitting on Mum's bed having a good cry. The nurse had wheeled my new brother's cot over my foot. Not to be outdone Rich joined in as well. I was very mystified because I knew that Mum had been in hospital with a broken leg before I was born, therefore broken legs or painful feet were to do with babies, so her leg must have been broken again to get baby Richard.
>
> I also remember at a later date an Australian Brown snake curled up in the fire place and me shouting for Mum. I knew that they were very nasty things and not to touch. Mum came in and banged a big stick to rouse the snake from its sleep. I can see it now uncoiling itself and slithering away. It was next seen making its way across the mantel shelf above the cooker. Mum knocked it off onto the fire and it sizzled to death.

Lyminster in Sussex would hold no reptilian terrors! There would also be no more alarming dust cloud storms which had terrified the living daylights out of young Richard and Polly Cooper. Polly was only four and half when the *SS Moreton Bay* left Port Melbourne in early 1931. She remembers clutching her cuddly polar bear as she was held aloft to wave to all the uncles and aunts from both sides of the family, Cooper and Metherall, who had come to the quay to see them off. Streamers were thrown down to the family throng below. Grasping them tight as the ship moved off with the hooting of the tugs, the streamers tautened and finally snapped in what was more than a symbolic breaking of ties with my Gran Cooper's six brothers and two sisters. They were heartstrings which could not be mended by the almost daily arrival of family mail from Australia over the ensuing decades. It would be a full 42 years before she returned to her native land.

The *Moreton Bay* made its way to England through the Suez Canal and arrived at Southampton on Monday 13th April 1931. Polly can recall stopping off at Port Said and buying a little leather purse with an embossed design of mountains and bamboo on the flap. The snap closure was covered by a tiny pink ivory elephant. It stayed with Polly throughout her days at Lyminster.

No one had worked harder to eke a living out of the virgin soil than Grandpa Cooper. By 1931, his farm had degenerated into huge rolling mounds and ridges of blown sand standing at least 100 feet in height and covered by eucalyptus trees. During the summer months the air quivered with the scorching heat which blazed down from the unbroken blue of crystal clear skies. In winter the dawns were sometime superb, great masses of cloud hanging low etched against the rising sun.

The Mallee, Northern Victoria

The area of Northern Victoria where Grandpa farmed was known as 'The Mallee'. This area comprised of about 11,000,000 acres adjoining the river Murray. It was regarded as an absolutely worthless desert incapable of being turned to agricultural account, although it became one of the principal areas settled by soldiers after 1918 as the land was divided by the Australian Government into farms of one square mile (640 acres).

The scrub land itself was comparatively easily cleared. Many years later, this clearance resulted in erosion on a grand scale, similar to the Dust Bowl in the Montana of the 1930s. The Mallee roller was a large hollow drum about eight or ten feet long and four feet in diameter. These rollers were pulled by teams of up to eight horses. Having been rolled the resultant sap-filled scrub was left to dry and then burned at a suitable time. After ploughing, huge roots, ranging in size from a couple to a hundred pounds in weight were collected and burned. Newly sown crops had to battle with weeds and rabbits in order to make any sort of headway, but the Mallee farmers, including Grandpa Cooper, prepared the earth and irrigated their wheat crops through the building of communal dams. It was in these dams that his young children, Polly and Richard, learnt to swim before they could walk.

The Browns and Coopers were moving to Lyminster from totally different circumstances. The contrast between the Cooper's farm in the Mallee, Northern Victoria, and the England of West Sussex was as stark as one can imagine. My grandmother was thrown into an almost alien culture of affluent Middle England far away from her large farming family back home in Australia.

Lyminster Guernseys

Cecil Cooper's official title of Manager meant that he oversaw every aspect of farm life, the centre of which would be the magnificent Guernsey herd. The original bull of the herd, Zena's Laddie, was a fiery beast! George

Carmen would later take charge of the prized animal and he told me in 1999 that he was nearly gored against the farm railings one morning, after the bull had proverbially got out of bed the wrong side! A portrait of Zena's Laddie was painted in 1947 by Frank Beresford, a friend of the Browns, who was later commissioned to paint *The Lying in State of King George VI*.

The first cow to arrive at Lyminster was christened Niobe, as she bellowed so incessantly for her offspring. Her athletic powers were such that she remained the only cow to have ever jumped the ha-ha at Lyminster! Niobe was followed by Stapleford Jess, who was duly registered in the Guernsey Herd Book. These were the bovine acorns which grew into an oak tree of a fine pedigree-attested herd, the equal of any in Southern England. Each cow had an individual name to match its character, a name more often than not associated with the extended family. Hence Linda's Pride and Polly's Pride were named after Linda and Polly Cooper. From 1931, this remained a tradition right through the years, including the family's move to Somerset in 1946, until the herd was sold in January 1968. Today, the EEC's Common Agricultural Policy would struggle to cope with such individuality!

Chapter 4

Auntie Vi and Uncle Cecil Brown

You will remember that my great-aunt, Vi Brown, was an idealist, brought up in the great tradition of Methodist nonconformism Her strict moral code was exemplified in 1912, when after the birth of her son John a letter from Germany was received offering contraceptive advice. Her reaction was both forthright and legendary, ripping up the advertisement before throwing the fragments into the waste paper bin. She accused the advertiser, Ley, who was later controller of forced labour in the First World War, of introducing a subtle way of undermining England's national stamina and integrity! Vi regarded physical intercourse purely as a means of procreation – if it wasn't that, then prostitution should be regarded as an honourable profession. She did not regard marriage as a lifelong licence to mate.

Daphne Byrne provides a pen picture of my great-aunt. Daphne was a Land Girl in the Second World War. The daughter of a Royal Navy Captain, she used to stay at Lyminster House and kept in contact with the Browns until Vi's death in 1970. Daphne wrote to me in April 1999 and provided a wonderfully atmospheric description of her great friend:

Short, round and a ball of fire. A great and enthusiastic motivator and everything opposite to Mr Brown. A member of the Fabian Society. A great organiser and immensely kind and hospitable. She did not inspire fear or awe but respect for her energy and a slight shrinking into one's shell; the kind of feeling you have when someone was going to slap you in the back! But this may well be a great injustice and I was shy and gormless in those days. Of course you went along with all she so kindly activated on our behalf and we were really thankful to the Browns as life in farm cottages was pretty bleak after a hard day in the fields and frankly, we were cheap labour.

Mrs Brown always took an interest in the younger generation and helped them in any way she could.

Great-aunt Brenda, Grandpa Cooper and Vi Brown's youngest sister, played the role of maiden aunt of the Cooper clan with enthusiastic glee. She was assigned to look after my great-grandmother in old age and became unofficial governess to all of us great-nephews and nieces, visiting us in turn throughout the year. On the death of Vi Brown in 1970, Brenda wrote:

A Maker of 'Home' and Gardens.

The physical and practical work involved in being this Vi put chiefly in the latter; but the spiritual and idealistic she contributed to both.

An individualist with an exceptional brain, a tender heart, an insatiable desire to prove by reason, the matters of Life and Death. A thinker ahead of her times and with that possibly a little impatient of slower thinkers, who must reach their own conclusions at their own pace (who knows, however, that the slower need the impetus of the faster to help to them arrive at all!!)

A gifted worker in needlework and creator of beautiful gardens.

A lover of the Truth and an enemy of anything sham. Generous to a degree.

1939 Vi Brown (nee Cooper) in her
beloved garden at Lyminster House.

Vi was the driving force behind the wonderful cricket at Lyminster in the 1930s. Together with her husband CNB they provided outstanding cricketing facilities, a level playing field if ever there was one, and open house hospitality to all cricketers at Lyminster. The large rooms quickly became temporary dormitories for the cricketers in the summer months. In cricket, Violet believed, lay all the values and traditions of English society itself, a game which represented a higher morality than any other. The aesthetic appeal of cricket had no equal, especially when played in beautiful surroundings such as Lyminster. The level playing field of Lyminster House was created in reality by the Browns' gardener, Mr Asplin. In order to learn the secrets of his trade, he was sent away to the County Ground at Horsham. He very quickly produced a batting strip and outfield the equal of anywhere in Sussex: indeed within three years the Sussex Club and Ground XI were playing regular fixtures at Lyminster House. The only club ground to rival Lyminster in quality can only be

North Perrott in South Somerset, my home club. Tom Parkman is Perrott's Mr Asplin, producing magnificent batting wickets and billiard table outfields. This Thomas Hardy figure of South Somerset, is testimony that tradition does live on, even if examples are few and far between.

Vi Brown was highly intelligent, had great energy and vision, but if crossed, her reaction could be volcanic. Auntie Vi was an outstanding sportswoman. Cricket was her first love. Remember, she had played for Girton, Cambridge in the Edwardian era after leaving the North London Collegiate School for Girls until the age of 20. It is hard for some folk today to believe that women played sport during those days. A Cambridge hockey Blue and leading goal scorer at the University, she also competed in the English Ladies Golf Championships at Cooden Beach in 1924, her 9 handicap entitling her to enter at a course very near to the Browns' holiday home at Yapton, near the Sussex coast. Auntie Vi was a regular partner of the great Harry Vardon at the South Herts Club and they regularly competed in the 'Bystander Trophy' for Professional and Lady golfer. Vardon was the professional at the South Herts club where both the Browns were members. Vi and Cecil would often take golfing holidays to Scotland, playing some of the great courses such as Machrie on the Isle of Islay and St Andrews.

Vi also believed that the concept of the Virgin Birth of Christ implied that man's share in the creative act might be impure. This she resented on man's behalf. After the birth of her son John in 1912, Vi was true to her word and remained celibate. Vi had married CNB two years earlier. He was the youngest of five brothers, the sons of the Rev. J. M. Brown, a Methodist Missionary to India, and Mary Kilner. CNB was a very shy, almost timid man, who preferred to merge into the background rather than take centre stage He was content to see others enjoying fulfilling lives, very often as a direct result of his benevolence. This genuine kindness of heart and spirit was the essence of his character, traits which were reflected in the many branches of Methodism in the Brown family, and amongst all those who intermarried with the Coopers in Finchley before the First World War. His love of cricket had blossomed at Kingswood School, Bath, which was a Methodist foundation started by John Wesley. Daphne Byrne always remembers CNB in the following terms:

> Think of a charming, quiet, self-effacing, perfect English Gentleman and you have Mr Brown. He was slight, not very tall and one of the nicest men you were likely to meet in a lifetime. Extremely hospitable and not obviously around.

Uncle Cecil's obituary in the 1961 Kingswood School magazine reflects Daphne Byrne's view of the man:

> Son and grandson of distinguished Methodist Wesleyan Missionaries, he started on the lowest level at Lloyds, but soon became a partner in a successful syndicate. Modest and reserved almost to a fault, he was surprised to learn on his retirement after 47 years at Lloyds, in what esteem he was held by all who had worked with or under him. No one better exemplified the qualities of integrity, honesty and courtesy which have made Lloyds famous throughout the world. His unfailing generosity and kindliness put many in his debt. His retiring nature gave him no taste for public affair, but throughout his long and active life, he kept up a lively interest in Kingswood and all its doings, as four nephews (3 Browns and one Cooper) knew best of all. A splendid games player himself, it was perhaps the school's sporting achievements that most interested him and his memories of Homeric struggles with Monkton Combe or Bristol Grammar School gave him pleasure to the end.

Sir Richard Doll, the medical pioneer who first linked smoking with cancer, wrote to Vi after CNB's death:

I have always felt that Cecil was a personal friend. We may, I know, have appeared an ungrateful lot in our early 20s when we used to share your hospitality at Lyminster, but I think you know by now how much pleasure those visits gave us all. I will always be grateful to Cecil working on the wicket (which we took for granted) and if I can't repay it in some respect, by doing the same for somebody else, it certainly won't be for want of trying. It will be that the model was too difficult to copy.

Sir Richard Doll's medical career has benefited mankind a million times over. He is still working at the age of 88, producing reports on the link between cancer in young children and proximity to pylons.

The other Trifler who remembered Cecil so clearly and articulately is Francis Pagan:

He was one of the most entirely loveable men I have ever met, and I of all the people have good reason to know the kindness as a thing even above his generosity, which was great ...The Lyminster years must seem long ago to you now, but for any Trifler they are a fresh and unforgettable memory and always in the picture (though you had to look closely into the background at times) was the trim, brisk, neat, courteous figure of CNB...to all of us he was, even with our differences in age, a personal friend. When it came to my turn to play host in my own house I am sure I tried to model my behaviour on his, though I doubt if I ever could match it.

CNB's generosity included paying my father's fees at Kingswood School, Bath. It would delight him no end to know that the Cooper name still prevails at Kingswood today. There were many Methodist Missionaries in the Brown family, but in 1999 Sir Ralph Kilner Brown, an ex-High Court Judge and Cecil Brown's nephew, told me the amazing tale of another branch of the Brown family. One chap was press-ganged in Edinburgh in the nineteenth century: the ship sailed round the coasts of Scotland and Wales before the individual in question jumped ship in the middle of the Bristol Channel. From there, he went on to build much of Porlock and Watchet!

In 1926 Aunty Vi joined the Labour party as a form of support to the workers involved in the General Strike. Perhaps she never fully realised that it was easy to hold egalitarian principles if you were more than comfortably off. However, she spread her money freely around both the family and any community in which she lived – her idealistic views did much good in every community in which she lived. Her eccentricity is exemplified when on a cruise to the West Indies in 1936, she won the ship's fancy dress competition, taking the stage in full boxing regalia! Other contestants were adorned as Marie Antoinette or dressed in flowing Elizabethan robes. They could not quite comprehend her desire to pursue a self-deprecating mockery of both herself and the stereotypical nature of such contests!

Chapter 5

'The solemn trifler with his boasted skill'
William Cowper, Westminster School 1742–49

That wonderful writer Hugh de Selincourt wrote in his famous book *The Cricket Match*:

I think you'd ask a bloke to put his bloody marriage off for a game of cricket.

This extract certainly captured the thoughts of one Trifler from Lyminster in the 1930s who went on the annual tour to Scotland while his second son was being born!

During the 1930s, my father's cousin John Brown would battle many times on the cricket field against de Selincourt, John as captain of the Lyminster Triflers CC and Hugh leading Storrington CC. The Lyminster Triflers, the family cricket team, always gathered for a day's cricket in their splendid pink, green and black striped blazers. My grandfather still wore his up to his death at the age of 79 in 1973.

Cricket, good manners and friendly vicars?

Alan Campbell – Johnson, a founder member of the Triflers(later Lord Mountbatten's Press Attaché) with Polly and Richard Cooper, 1933.
Lyminster House.

"The Triflers", 1933 left to right; Frances Pagan, Alan Campbell-Johnson, John Alderson, Bobby Angelo, Sir Richard Doll, John Brown, John Bune, Sir John Latey, Eric Bompas, Jack Rich, Major General Errol Lonsdale, Michael Broadhurst.

"Can WE bat Vicar ?!!" The Reverend Duval with the Cooper children, Lyminster, 1934.

Lyminster House in the 1930s was a world of good

manners and friendly vicars, although the village's portly, scarlet-cheeked Rev. Duval could be a frightening apparition when short of food for any length of time! Everything that the Reverend did tended to be done with excessive zeal and enthusiasm. He would become totally immersed in a game of tip-and-run cricket, always unwilling to yield the strike even in the context of a game against the young Cooper children Polly and Richard! He would bat for bloody hours on end, or so it seemed! The simple act of bustling down Church Lane was a comic picture, hand on mortar board with the tassel bobbing, usually somewhere between a walking run and a running walk in a desire to get to Matins. Duval was delightfully eccentric, a character trait which, sadly, has all but disappeared from the English country scene.

John Brown's Triflers' Cricket Club

In 1931, the priority was the renovation of the house, farm and cottage where Cecil Cooper's family would live. John Brown, son of CNB and Vi, founded 'The Triflers Cricket Club' the following year in 1932. As a young man, he was tremendously enthusiastic about everything he did, and sometimes fiery, but he never lost a friend. In time he would mature into a great Headmaster. Membership of the club had to be made predominantly of the Old Boys and pupils of Westminster School in London. Founder members John Brown, Francis Pagan, Alan Campbell-Johnson and Jock Engleheart had remembered that in the eighteenth century an unofficial and irreverent Westminster magazine had appeared called The Trifler. Their motto was taken from a Westminster poet, William Cowper, who wrote 'The Solemn Trifler with his Boasted Skill'. The Triflers regularly strengthened the Lyminster House village side, which comprised of local players.

They were as much idealists as the Brown family were. The Triflers were not merely a group of spoilt public schoolboys playing cricket. They had rejected the traditional suburban London clubs and the 'gin and it' brigade, to quote a surviving Trifler. Lyminster House was an oasis where they could almost play out a Corinthian fantasy, playing the game in an attacking classic form.

The Triflers were thus born at Lyminster in 1932 from the 1931 vintage, with their successors progressing into the team throughout the 30s. The *Cricketer Annual* for 1932 reviewed Westminster School's 1931 season:

> M. Broadhurst was a beautiful stylist, and could be relied on to make fine strokes on the off-side; J. S. Brown could make some good strokes, but was unsound; A. C. Johnson and F. E. Pagan were a sound opening pair.
>
> With the exception of A. C. Johnson, who is still too slow through the air to trouble good batsmen, non of the bowlers could keep a length.

My father's cousin John Brown was a cavalier batsman who never 'played for his average', he was as likely to throw his wicket away with a reckless shot as smash a quick-fire 50. As a cover point fieldsman, he was absolutely top class, patrolling the off-side like Jonty Rhodes today.

All the Triflers were in their own way idealists, although Vi Brown clearly remembers one who in the early days of the team left his shoes out to be polished and rang a bell for room service! Lyminster House was not that sort of place, the Browns did not hold such values. Auntie Vi is sure that her husband CNB did the necessary chore, and perhaps the message got home to the individual concerned. Examination of their subsequent careers proves the point though that the Triflers were idealistic, and turned their backs on many of the traditional aspects of upper-middle-class life. They had rejected the ethos of the big suburban cricket clubs and welcomed the chance to play their own brand of cricket as they had learnt it at Westminster. They found a spiritual home at nonconformist Lyminster.

Grandpa Cooper ran the Lyminster House village side which played at weekends, mainly comprised of local players and visiting Triflers down from University. In the summer of 1931, John Brown left Westminster School and entered Trinity College, Cambridge, along with his great friend Francis Pagan. John and Francis were joined on the first Trifler committee by Alan Campbell-Johnson who was studying Modern History at Christ Church, Oxford, under the brilliant tutorship of John Masterman; Richard Doll, a medical student at St Thomas' Hospital, London, later voted by the *Guardian* in 1998 as one of the twentieth century's most influential men; and Jock Engleheart, a concert pianist and conductor. These four joined their fellow ex-Westminsters in the first official photograph, namely John Alderson, Bobbie Angelo, John Bune, John Brinsmead Latey, Eric Bompas, Jack Rich, Erroll Lonsdale, Ian Munro and Michael Broadhurst.

In the summer of 1932 the *Cricketer* magazine gave weekly accounts of matches in the Home Counties. John Brown, it appears, played nearly every day in that 1932 summer whilst on vacation from Trinity College, either for the Old Westminsters XI or for the famous Sussex Martlets. He went straight into an OW's match against Wimbledon after a two day Martlets fixture versus Old Brightonians. The Old Westminsters played against Wimbledon on July 31st, 1932. That doyen of all cricket writers, Mr E. W. 'Jim' Swanton, scored 112 for Wimbledon that day. John Brown scored 27 in contributing to a very rare tie, with the scores level on 216 apiece. Jim Swanton, CBE, died on January 22nd, 2000.

The day before his death, I received the following letter from him outlining the fact he had agreed to help me with this book:

The Cricketer International
From The President,
E. W. Swanton C. B. E.
January 19th, 2000

Dear Mr Cooper,

I remember you writing last year and I'm so pleased that your book is to be published. Unfortunately I am dictating from The Chaucer Hospital, Canterbury – hence my secretary's signature to this letter.

My recollection is that I made 100 twice, possibly in successive years against the Old Westminsters and I think, it must have been for Wimbledon. I don't remember anything much more although I do recall Sir Richard Doll and Alan Campbell-Johnson and Judge Stocker and Anthony Craxton who was once entrusted with the Queen's Speech and lost it at Sandringham.

I hope I will not be here too long and once I am back home I might possibly be able to help if you cared to ring. In any case all good luck with the book.

    Yours sincerely,
    D. Waite
    p. p. E. W. Swanton

Jim Swanton wrote about cricket right up to his death.

He penned 23 cricket books, spent countless hours at the microphone and wrote most of his newspaper articles for the *Daily Telegraph*. John Major described him as 'one of the great cricket writers of the twentieth century'. David Gower said, 'Jim has been a legend for a long time. What was outstanding was his immense recall and his acute sense of what is good about the game and its moral values.' He had something of a reputation of being 'Old School', but it is precisely these values which will sustain the principles of the tradition which makes the game so unique. Swanton was a committed Christian and was not frightened to stand up against the very establishment he was often accused of perpetuating. His condemnation of apartheid was a refreshing comparison to the quiet acceptance of a regime which banned Basil D'Oliveira from touring South Africa with the MCC in the late 60s. Many people in the game were content to maintain links with South Africa. Simon Heffer, writing in the *Sunday Telegraph* on January 23rd, 2000 stressed that:

> Jim was in many ways the sort of man foreigners construct when they caricature the English, though that was to his credit. He sincerely believed that cricket was a metaphor for life, that it should be the example of the straight bat. As he became older, these were values that began to seem ancient; though not to him, nor to his loyal readers.

Jim Swanton had a reputation for encouraging young cricket writers. His spirit lives on and he would have wholeheartedly approved of the cricket played at Lyminster House in the 30s. No team reflected the true values of English cricket more than the Lyminster Triflers in the 1930s. If cricket is indeed a metaphor for England's green and pleasant land, a triumph of civilisation over barbarity, enmeshed in the centuries long traditions of fair play, then the Lyminster House ground stood out like a shining beacon, a monument to all things which a decent 1930s Englishmen believed in. We could have hardly challenged Germany to play a series of test matches in 1939! Junker values would have been rather compromised by the rituals and traditions associated with the game! Were the great victories of the Franco-Prussian war won on the playing fields of schools in Berlin? Perhaps not.

Open House at Lyminster

As the decade progressed many players from opposition teams were recruited, very often to play on the annual tour to Scotland. The hospitality offered by the Browns included putting up as many as 15 Triflers in the largest bedroom during the annual cricket fortnight in August and September. From then on, it became known as the 'Trifler's Dormitory'. Maud Cooper, Vi Brown's cousin, made sure they were regally fed. Francis Pagan remembers that there was a tennis court and billiards room – even a cricket net was contrived between an alleyway beside the ground. In the evening there were other choices. A pub on the seafront at Littlehampton attracted the restless: the Browns only offered beer during dinner to their cricketing guests, never spirits – a semi-strict prohibition policy for all visitors!

Most of the Triflers were content to sit on the red leather armchairs or on the floor in the hall, listening to the Proms on the radio, or taking it in turns to play bridge with their hosts the Browns. A peaceful, civilised scene. The first match was played against Littlehampton on September 1st, 1932, the home ground at Lyminster not being ready until the following year. The Triflers were thus born, embarking on a short but momentous era of English country house cricket, until the ravages of the

1939–45 war took so many of the team, and the Browns left Lyminster after a very unpleasant family scandal, the nature of which unfolds later in the book. Today it would not even warrant the turning of heads!

Chapter 6

1932 – 'Ale and home-made apple pie'
The Norfolk Arms, Steyning

Letters from Australia

Cecil Cooper regularly corresponded with his solicitor, Herbie Blair, back in the dust-bowl of Manangatang. There was much business regarding his old farm to sort out, but the letters also discussed news of the Mallee, the latest cricketing views and political affairs in Europe, an enduring passion of Cecil Cooper's.

There had been a typhoid scare in the Manangatang area in 1932; the Australian Government had cut the old age pension to 15 shillings per week in line with maternity benefit reductions; gangs of unemployed were put to work catching rabbits in the outback and repairing roads. The worldwide depression hit Australia as hard as anywhere. Herbie Blair, a straight-talking Aussie, also included the following:

> I often think of the brave and terrible fight you and Linda put up in the Mallee, tears of sweat, blood and anguish. You did as well as any anyone could do and better than hundreds of others, leaving behind a good name and holding the respect of everyone.

There had also been a tabloid newspaper rumour that the country was being overrun by the Japanese. Herbie Blair ironically informed Cecil Cooper that the government's 'White Australia' policy had made it more 'British' than any other country in the world! The curse of xenophobia was no real threat to the human soul in Australia, but in Germany, it began to rumble like a bad case of national indigestion. Nobody expected that in seven years time another war would start. Cecil Cooper was to keep Herbie Blair informed as to the state of Germany's political health throughout the 30s.

Nazi rumblings

1932 was the beginning of the Nazi Party's rise to power. I don't think that anybody in the early cricket teams at Lyminster would have predicted the invasion of Poland in 1939. Hitler was uniting all the nationalistic, Volkish and right wing groups in the country in 1932. He welded together the working classes and the Junker classes into one body. The belief that Adolf Hitler took power without the support of the German people is often mistakenly held. The truth is that the displaced urban masses voted for him in their millions, the abhorrent Nazi ideology striking a deep chord in the soul of people after their experience of events in the 1920s and early 30s. The Versailles Treaty had emasculated Germany's spiritual soul. Unemployment, war reparations, a loss of national identity and inflation made an irrational ideology attractive to the masses, for these were irrational times. There was no real history of democracy in Germany and the Weimar Republic did not fit with Germany's tradition of 'Blood and Iron' espoused by Bismarck in the 1890s. The Nazis tapped into the 'Volkish' roots of the nation, the romantic and biological attachment to the blood and soil of Germany. Nazism assuaged the masses' need for aggression as their outlet for pent up anger built up since 1918. The Nazis were, in essence, the synthetic product of all the collective malaise of the post-WW1 years in Germany. A bitterly strident country was united through hatred, exemplified in anti-Semitism, the long established bigotry and racism which had always been deep-rooted in Germany.

The Nazi Party chose Hitler as their Presidential candidate on February 22nd, and although defeated by Hindenburg on March 13th, Hitler manipulated his way into power, cynically abusing the democratic process in Germany. Consequently, the political thugs of the SS and SA were banned. The Nazis only won elections in four states in the April elections.

By July 31st, they had won an incredible 230 seats in the Reichstag. Hitler manipulated and destroyed democracy through a combination of secret deals and coalitions with other xenophobic groups. There were no mounting of the barricades or storming of palaces in the 1917 St Petersburg sense, only exploitation of existing democratic procedures which had no place in 'real' German historic experience. The road to Armageddon became a one-way street in 1932.

The political chaos in Germany was a long way from the green and pleasant land of West Sussex. The Guernsey herd was developing nicely, thick cream milk becoming the staple diet of the Cooper family for the next 36 years, until the herd was finally sold at Lyminster Farm, Crewkerne in January 1968, one of the last commercial Guernsey concerns in Southern England.

The first match

On September 1st, 1932, The Triflers' Cricket Club played their long awaited first game, away against Littlehampton C.C. just two miles down the road from their Lyminster base.

September 1st, 1932

Littlehampton CC			Triflers' CC		
F.A. Hawkins		24	F.E. Pagan		25
A.C. Somerset		2	J.S. Brown		3
W.F. Becker		4	R.H. Angelo		10
B.W. Marshall		21	M. Broadhurst		21
J.C. Bune (Trifler)		78	I.K. Munro		12
J. Alderson (Trifler)		46	G.C.E. Oxer		20
H.K. Dixon		3	E.H.G. Lonsdale		5
C.C. Cooper (Trifler)		14	J.B. Latey		0
M.D. Mann		1	E.A. Bompas		8
C.J. Summers	N/O	4	J.E. Rich		4
G. Blunt, Jnr		0	W.R.S. Doll	NO	11
Extras		2	Extras		2

Total 173   **Total** 151
F.E. Pagan 6–56   F.A. Hawkins 5–80

Littlehampton CC won by 22 runs

A very good all-round performance by founder member Francis Pagan was not enough to avert defeat. John Bune, a Trifler guesting for Littlehampton, produced a match-winning innings which saw the home team to victory. Pagan was renowned for his technically correct batting skills, opening the innings from this first game in 1932 up until the final fixture against Ashtead in August 1940. He opened the batting for Suffolk CCC for three years before the war.

Major-General Errol Lonsdale

Trifler Errol Lonsdale's later career as a Major-General in the RASC reached a peak when he was appointed 'Transport -in-Chief' in 1966, after spending two years as ADC to the Queen. In his early Trifler years, he was the only player to be entrusted with Vi Brown's Daimler. This was very appropriate for a man who became Chairman of the Institute of Advanced Motorists in 1971! Vi Brown must have known a safe driver when she saw one. Her own son John had a terrible reputation for driving at great speed, usually on the wrong side of the road, although, it has to be said, he never had an accident. Whilst working in the War Office under Winston Churchill's reign as Prime Minister between 1951 and 1953, Errol Lonsdale had to organise transport for General De Gaulle to be taken to Chequers. In 1997, he delighted in recounting to me that the driver allocated to the job ended up delivering the French General to a pub in Buckinghamshire of the same name! Luckily, the French leader took it in good humour and no lasting damage was done to Anglo-French relations! De Gaulle had already spent his career doing that!

Major-General Lonsdale was also President of the British Modern Pentathlon Association and was thrilled to preside over Great Britain's gold medal winning triumphs at the Olympic Games of 1972 and 1976.

Sir John Brinsmead Latey

John Latey became a famous High Court judge and is best known for producing the report which led to the age of majority being reduced in Britain from 21 to 18. Latey himself had personal misgivings over the decision, but after two years of general debate, he bowed to the consensus.

In 1987, he ruled in a test case brought about by the Government that a married couple were free to adopt a two-year-old girl conceived by the husband and a surrogate mother, who had been paid £5,000 to bear the child.

Latey was a contemporary of Alan Campbell-Johnson's at Christ Church, Oxford. After service in the war as a Lieutenant-Colonel in Cairo, he returned to a career in the Law. In 1952, he cooperated with his father on the 14th edition of *Latey on Divorce*. In 1964, he was appointed Master of the Bench at the Middle Temple. He became, like his father before him, an expert in divorce.

As a man Sir John Latey was much loved, being approachable, understanding and possessing a lovely sense of humour which often diffused awkward situations. Like fellow Trifler Rodney Smith, he became an expert bridge player in his later years.

Steyning Cricket Club

The last two games of the 1932 season were played against Steyning and Havant. For many Triflers their favourite fixture was Steyning, the lovely big ground tucked away behind the main street with a clear view of the Downs and Chanctonbury Ring. The Steyning team of the 1930s included players such as Sussex batsman Jack Eaton and the formidable C. J. 'Juggy' Holden, who later went as groundsman to the county ground at Horsham. Chris Breach, the captain, was a forthright character to match the Trifler's own explosive John Brown. Like many Triflers who played there, Holden did not come back after the war. Steyning's most popular player was the amiable Fred Laker who kept the Norfolk Arms opposite the old Grammar School. His wife's marvellous home-made apple tart would be washed down with quantities of ale from the hop fields of the neighbouring county of Kent. Francis Pagan particularly remembers the Steyning scorer, a courteous old gentleman who wore a black jacket and stiff white butterfly collar with the wonderful name of Mr E. A. F. Mould!

Village cricket has always thrown up the most eccentric and colourful men in terms of character or deed. Steyning's strike bowler was a man called Lockwood. His left arm ended in a stump which he covered with a little black glove, he had a cleft palate and a tinderbox temper. Lockwood also bowled frighteningly fast! Rodney Smith (later Baron Smith of Marlow, President of the Royal College of Surgeons, who died in 1998), the Trifler's opening bat and renowned hooker of quick bowling, was once bowled by him whilst in the middle of his backlift!

Friendly relations were also enjoyed with the Havant team who were blessed with such players as ex-Sussex batsman Ted Bowley, Philip Blake and his son John.

September 10th, 1932

Havant CC			Triflers' CC		
E.H. Bowley		43	F.E. Pagan		6
L.V. Glare		8	J. Alderson		16
G.W.S. Brown		64	J.C. Bune		2
P. Blake		9	M. Broadhurst	N. O.	56
R.J. Gates		32	R.H. Angelo		1
G. Bridger	N. O.	15	J.S. Brown		2
H.G. Boswell	N. O.	0	I.K. Munro		15
C.E.R. Smith	D.		A. C-Johnson		24
W.B. Mason	N.		E.H.G. Lonsdale		7
J.S. Gates	B		W.R.S. Doll	N. O.	0
P. Clark	AT		J.E. Rich	D.N. .	
Total declared	174 for 6 wickets		**Total**	132 for 8 wickets	
A. C-Johnson 3–57			H. G. Boswell 3–44		

Match Drawn

Ted Bowley, the Blakes and the Rev. Jessop

Ted Bowley was a living legend in the County of

Sussex. In 1929, Bowley had scored 2,359 runs and taken 90 wickets in his most prolific season, including 280 not out against Gloucestershire, putting on 368 for the first wicket with John Langridge. That year young John Blake appeared, who later became a Trifler shortly before winning a Cambridge Blue in 1939, distinguishing himself in the match against Oxford at Lords. He also played County cricket for Hampshire.

The Rev. G. L. O. Jessop, veritable son of the famous Gilbert 'The Croucher', did not figure in this match, but the following year hit four 4s in five balls off the bowling of Alan Campbell-Johnson and took 6 wickets for 47 runs in the game. Jessop won a Cambridge Blue in 1927 and had a brief first-class career with Hampshire in 1933, before playing for Minor Counties' Cambridgeshire in 1936.

The Trifler's first season ended with them playing five games, drawing three and losing two matches. The fresh young players, recently embarked in careers at various Universities, would grow to love their cricket at Lyminster during their long vacations. Even after graduating, they continued to make the short annual summer pilgrimage to CNB and Mrs B's (as they were affectionately known) cricketing oasis. In addition to the Steyning and Havant fixtures, further matches at Bognor, Storrington and Worthing were played as part of a Triflers' 'Cricket Week'. It became a firm fixture on the Sussex cricket calendar. For other matches at Lyminster, touring or otherwise homeless sides such as the Sussex Martlets and Sussex Club and Ground XI were top attractions.

Chapter 7

1933 – 'For King and Country?' – Alan Campbell-Johnson and Francis Pagan

Mission with Mountbatten

In June 1997, I began researching the background to this story and wrote a hopeful letter to Alan Campbell-Johnson who immediately put me in touch with Francis Pagan, another old Trifler and founder member. He had taught at Classics at Epsom College before and after the war, became a publisher from 1964 to 1970, prior to being appointed as Public Relations Officer for the Slimbridge Wildlife Trust. Francis then wrote travel guides to Provence, Burgundy and the Greek Islands, doing so well into his 80s. They were both very much cut in the mould of my Great-uncle Cecil Brown and Grandpa Cooper, who were dignified English gentlemen with a mellow warmth, surrounding a sage-like inner self.

Francis and Alan had been great friends of my father's cousin John Brown who started the Triflers team. They had all left Westminster School in 1931, before going on to Oxbridge: John and Francis to Trinity College, Cambridge and Alan to Christ Church, Oxford. A fellow pupil, the infamous spy and MI5 double agent Kim Philby, had taken the same Westminster-Trinity path in the same year. The similarities ended there though! Over a splendid lunch in London, we reminisced and exchanged news covering many decades. Alan remarked that he was still mortified at Philby's defection and that he must have been a triple agent! Francis recounted in minute detail the events and incidents surrounding both the cricket and my family at Lyminster House. He had also written articles on the Triflers for their 50th and 60th anniversaries in *Sussex Life* and for the *Elizabethan*, the Westminster School magazine.

As keeper of the extended family tree, I provided information about relations not seen by Alan and Francis for years. It was clear that both these men had loved their time at Lyminster House. Francis handed over the most wonderful calfskin leather score book, which was enclosed in a box of the same material, fixture cards and other artefacts. The turning of each page of this magnificent book uncovered many Triflers who went on to became famous men. In my hands was a piece of country house cricket history and in a sense a piece of lost England.

Alan was a useful right-handed batsman, but his greatest strength was his slow left-arm bowling. 'Slow through the air, fast off the bat!' he delighted in telling me. Such modesty was typical of the man who gave up the chance of an Oxford Cricket Blue in order to pursue a career (following in the wake of Beverly Nichols) as a writer whilst studying History at Christ Church College, guided by the brilliant mind of John Masterman, who would ironically play the main role in the last cricket match played by the Triflers in 1940.

The Oxford Union Debate, 1933

Alan's first book was called *Growing Opinions* (1935) and was based on interviews with 16 of his contemporaries. He wrote this after interviewing 16 of his contemporaries and attending the notorious debate at the Oxford Union in 1933 in which the vote (275 to 173) went in favour of not fighting for 'King and Country'. It was on February 9th, 1933, that David Graham had devised and seconded the notorious motion which specifically read, 'That this House will in no circumstances fight for its King and Country'. The result caused outrage amongst the Establishment. The *Daily Telegraph* appealed to 'decently minded young Oxford' to reverse it. The record of the debate was torn from the minute book. Graham rewrote it from memory.

The whole rumpus was meant to have encouraged Hitler to run amok over the Versailles Treaty, knowing that Britain did not have the stomach to fight another war. There is no evidence that the debate had any effect on Hitler at all. David Graham was not a pacifist but an individual who enjoyed causing controversy. The fallout from the debate, though, lasted for many years. During the war, John Masterman, Alan Campbell-Johnson's old tutor at Christ Church, Oxford (later Sir John Masterman, Provost of Worcester College), came face to face with the man whom he thought to be responsible for luring the Oxford undergraduates into overreacting in order to create a huge controversy. C. E. M. Joad was having dinner at the Dorchester, one of 16 guests of Victor Cazalet. Masterman, who was working in MI5 at the time (the details of which are discussed later in this book) and never forgave Joad for his part in the debate, asked to sit as far away from Joad as possible! During the conversational exchanges, Joad's self-opinionated outbursts on economic policy were soundly put down by other guests, making the evening a resounding success since he left early. Masterman was to have the final say in the closing chapter of Triflers Cricket Club in 1940.

Hitler becomes Chancellor

The 1933 Oxford debate did touch a raw nerve in the nation, however. Many did not want to fight another destructive and cruel war, particularly if it were perceived as pointless: memories of the Western Front trenches were far too recent and painful. The rise of Hitler's Nazi Party was a factor which as long as it didn't threaten British sovereignty or territory could be an issue confined to the European mainland. In1933, it was far too early even to contemplate another war, and there was also the small matter of Britain not being able to defend her Empire, let alone fight a major European war.

It was on January 30th that Adolf Hitler became German Chancellor. The Nazis quickly acted to facilitate their totalitarian policies, leaving the tattered remnants of Weimar democracy in ashes as the Reichstag building burnt to the ground on February 27th, set on fire by Nazi Brownshirts, but blamed on the Communist opposition. On March 23rd, 1933 they suppressed all German trade unions. The Nazis further clenched their grip on the German nation by banning all political parties in opposition to them on July 14th. This was the build-up to the massive torchlight rallies in the city of Nuremberg in early September.

'Peace Offerings' and a career with Mountbatten

Alan Campbell-Johnson's second book arrived in 1936, a year after he came down from Oxford. *Peace*

Offerings was a more ambitious enterprise, a series of interviews on war and peace with famous people of the day including Lloyd George, Aldous Huxley and Noel Coward.

Alan Campbell-Johnson's career reached a peak when he was appointed as Lord Mountbatten of Burma's press attaché during the Partition of India in 1947. Between 1937 and 1940 he had been unpaid secretary to Sir Archibald Sinclair, leader of the Liberal Party. It was Sinclair, by then Air Minister, who recommended him for the post of Press Officer for Mountbatten's new command at Combined Operations. Alan had volunteered for the RAF in 1939. When Mountbatten was made Supreme Commander in South East Asia in 1943, he took Alan Campbell-Johnson with him. He was made responsible for keeping the official war diaries, and spent two years flying around the war zone, trying to salvage material for the archives.

After the war, Campbell-Johnson stayed with Mountbatten (the last Viceroy and then the first Governor-General of India) and from March 1947 to June 1948 was press attaché during the difficult days of partition. *Mission with Mountbatten* was Alan Campbell-Johnson's thorough and detailed record of his time in India, which he later used to defend Mountbatten from blame regarding the blood-bath that followed partition. The violence was never trivialised by Campbell-Johnson, who escaped unscathed in Delhi when the motorcar in which he was travelling was shot at by a military patrol. The Sikh driver was killed and the Deputy Military Secretary to the Governor-General was injured. In 1950, Alan stood unsuccessfully for a second time as Parliamentary Candidate for Salisbury.

Alan Campbell-Johnson's Memorial Service, February 1998

Since our meeting, Alan has sadly died. I attended his memorial service, which was a celebration of his life in which he both helped make and saw history made. The wonderful choral music at St James's Church in Piccadilly provided a fitting backdrop to a spiritually uplifting occasion. Bach, Handel and Brahms filled the air. Vivaldi's *Gloria* and Mozart's *Alleluia* provided a spiritual crescendo, performed to the highest musical standards. Also present at the service that day were the Countess of Burma, David and Lady Pamela Hicks, Michael Portillo, and the famous historian Sir Martin Gilbert. These names reflected the wide and varied life which Alan had lived. His involvement in the India of 1947 must have been meteoric in every sense of the word. Alan described the years spent in Delhi with Mountbatten as the happiest of his working life. In the 1986 television series *Mountbatten: The Last Viceroy*, Alan was portrayed by the actor David Quiltor. Alan loved India and the Indian people and it is both appropriate and ironic that this book has reflected on the beauty of the nation's cricket. He played no small part in the partition of the country in 1947. Mistakes were made, but it was one of the most complex political jigsaws to construct. Different nationalities, cultures and religions provided a proverbial Molotov cocktail, ready to go off at any moment. The work is still not complete today as border disputes between India and Pakistan, allied to the Kashmir crisis, form an ongoing tense situation.

Alan was one of many Triflers who went on to make their mark on British history. They pushed back the barriers of medical science, innovated at the BBC in the field of sport and childrens' television, made a huge impact in the courts of justice, revolutionised education in 1944 or achieved the highest of ranks in Her Majesty's Armed Forces; they represented all the essential elements of the very Englishness which we may have lost in the modern world.

Return to the trenches

In 1933, my grandparents took their first holiday away from their new home at Lyminster. My grandfather took my grandmother to Flanders to visit the same trenches where he had safely delivered 24 messages in 24 hours whilst under heavy fire, winning the Russian Cross of St George in the process. It was a poignant scene, revisiting Ypres, the Menin Gate and Hill 60. The devastated square at Ypres was still in the process of being rebuilt. Still intact was Big Bertha, the gun which had bombarded the British coast. Little did he know that 11 years later, he would pass just to the south of the same area in 1944 in support of the D-Day armies as they marched towards Germany.

Bognor Regis CC and the Gilligan family

A second season of cricket was well under way at the Lyminster House ground, the highlight of which was the first of seven 1930s fixtures against the powerful Bognor Regis side, peppered with famous names in Sussex club cricket. One of the Gilligan family (the Rev. F. W.) put on 179 runs for the sixth wicket with a fine player called M. N. Ireland. Gilligan later became Headmaster of Wanganui Grammar School in New Zealand. An Oxford Blue in 1919, he played for Essex between 1919 and 1929. Gilligan received the OBE for his services to education in 1955. Gilligan and Ireland's partnership was matched by a stand of 150 for the Triflers' third wicket between Robin Edgar and Mike Broadhurst, the latter being a particularly stylish bat.

August 28th, 1933

Bognor Regis CC			The Triflers CC		
A Gadsdan		46	F.E. Pagan		3
N.E. Carter		0	J. Alderson		30
A.D. Hodges		34	J.S. Brown		5
P.T.R. Shelley		0	R.W. Edgar	N/O.	72
Rev. F.W. Gilligan		98	M. Broadhurst		72
H.M. Mullins		0	A. C-Johnson		
M.N. Ireland	N. O.	100	R.N. Heaton		
Col. Byrne	N. O.	1	J.O.H. Powell-Jones		
G.A. Anderson			C.C. Cooper		
J. Renniick			W.R.S. Doll		
C.B. French			J.E. Rich		
Total declared		286–6 wickets	**Total**	198–4 wickets	

J.E. Rich 3–62   C.B. French 3–36

Match Drawn

Storrington CC

Hugh de Selincourt's Storrington was a great bastion of Sussex village cricket. Francis Pagan recounts that de Selincourt, (as Gauvinier) and many of the players could be recognised as characters in that delightful book. In de Selincourt's book, Tillinghurst is in fact a pseudonym for his beloved Storrington. He wrote,

Tillingford lies in a hollow under the Downs, and climbs up the sides of the hill, like a pool risen to overflow its banks. The main street branches off in fingers up the sudden dip from the flat stretch that seemed, as you approached, to reach the foot of the downs.

The Cricket Match was an enduring account of the day in the life of Tillinghurst Cricket Club and their exploits in their local derby game, probably Steyning. De Selincourt writes beautifully, when skipper Gauvinier reflects on the day's deeds in defeating their local rivals as he cycles slowly back home

Even the cricket match was forgotten for a while as Gauvinier looked at the blaze of colour which celebrated the close of the day. He rode slowly, lingering as at a majestic rite. The whole vast sky glowed red and orange; the trees shone rosy in the reflected light which touched the hills. No breath of wind stirred the glowing stillness. His heart worshipped God and colour and life.

This wonderful account of the end of a perfect cricket day is echoed and reinforced by the magnificence of the Sussex countryside. Storrington was a quieter place than it is now, and the cricket field opposite the pond was surrounded by only a few cottages overlooking the Sussex farmland. The ground set problems for batsmen, as the pitch ran east and west in those days, and the side batting last had to cope with slow bowling tossed high into the setting sun, ideal conditions for the young Alan Campbell-Johnson to practise his cunningly flighted left-arm 'slows'!

On August 30th 1933, The Triflers set out to play first match against Hugh de Selincourt's team. The first ball was bowled at 3.45 pm, by 6.50 pm the match had finished with The Triflers winning by a margin of 58 runs.

August 30th, 1933

The Triflers			Storrington		
F.E. Pagan		47	W. Harmer		27
J. Alderson		32	C. Waller		6
J.S. Brown		8	C.I.A. Carr		20
R.W. Edgar		25	A. Ross		2
M. Broadhurst		5	C. Blomfield		13
W.R.S. Doll		17	M. Huffer		9
R.N. Heaton		10	D. Clarke		16
A. C-Johnson		5	H. de Selincourt		3
J.E. Rich		3	W. Williams		2
J.Powell-Jones	N. O.	4	J. Voisey		2
J.E. Gerrish	N. O.	5	G. Knowles	N. O.	0
Total	165–9 wickets declared		**Total**	107 all out	

H. de Selincourt 3–57   A. Campbell-Johnson 3–9
The Triflers won by 58 runs

At Lyminster, Mr Asplin was still busy preparing the home cricket wicket. Half the square had been levelled and turfed by a professional firm, who then killed the grass by an overdose of top-dressing, and so had to make a new effort late in 1933. That half always had a slight springiness as though resting on an air-cushion, but the half that Mr Asplin prepared and sowed was perfect. He nurtured the square with regal pride. Cricket wickets do not present themselves as ready to play without hour upon hour of cutting, rolling, feeding, spiking and weeding. The instant a match was finished, Asplin went out with a fork and pail of soil to lift up and fill in the heelmarks. The used wicket would be patched with grass from a special plot he had made himself. It was a labour of love because Mr Asplin was the sort of gardener who could not bear to lose a growing thing. The problem of the slope on the square was never overcome, falling rather sharply from the north. A bowling screen at that end was therefore impracticable because it would have had to be hung up in the trees. Luckily the background from that end was very clear.

A separate facility for visitors was soon added to the home pavilion in the form of a wooden building bought from a local cricket club in first class condition. It was fitted with a shower and a kitchen. A long roofed veranda ran the whole length of the front. This wonderful building became living accommodation for the next 60 years until it was sadly pulled down in the early 90s to make way for a new bungalow. This deed would not be allowed now, for today the whole of Lyminster has a preservation order attached to it. There is a long history associated with the old pavilion. Auntie Vi started a temporary school for evacuees in 1940. Various regiments set up machine-gun posts in it during the war years as well.

For the Lyminster Cricket Week in August, a huge marquee was erected. This completed a brilliant cricketing scene, perhaps only equalled in later years by the more famous Arundel Castle ground only three miles away.

August 31st, 1933

Steyning CC

H. Hicton		76
J.D. Clay		14
N.E. Adcock		10
C. Breach		6
C.J. (Juggy) Holden		37
F.B. Holden		18
F. Laker		33
C. Lewry		5
B. Coleman		0
K. Lindsay Stewart		0
S. Matthews	N. O.	0
Total	220 all out	

Triflers' CC

F.E. Pagan		10
J. Alderson		51
M. Broadhurst		82
J.S. Brown		1
R.N. Heaton		0
W.R.S. Doll		39
R.W. Edgar	N. O.	14
A. C-Johnson	N. O.	19
J.O.H. Powell-Jones	D.	
C.C. Cooper	N.	
J.E. Rich	B.	
Total	222 for 6 wickets	

F.E. Pagan 3–16   F.B. Holden 4–90

Triflers' CC won by 4 wickets

Chapter 8

1934 – 'Fairy godparents wanted!'

Lyminster House became the centre of one of Aunty Vi's social work projects concerning the Isle of Dogs. Poor families from the Millwall area of London came for an annual day out, very often bringing a cricket team to play the Lyminster House village side.

An advertisement in an edition of the *Times* in 1931 had asked for

…fairy godparents to send boys and girls to the Military Tournament.

Vi Brown sent a 10 shilling note to the Sub-Warden of Docklands Settlement No. 2, a Mr Kimberley. At face value it would be easy to accuse Vi Brown of benevolence from a safe distance, without having to take real action which meant more than the relatively simple act of putting one's hand in one's pocket. What resulted was far more than a simple act of patronage and brought the families from the Docklands of Millwall and the Isle of Dogs into the opulent surroundings of Lyminster House and its environs. What is more, Vi Brown maintained this link well into the war, corresponding with families who visited.

The amazing thing about the Docklands Project with

which Vi Brown got involved was that it was based on 'self-help', a concept and initiative seen today as modern! The Docklands Settlement No. 2 lay alongside the Millwall Recreation Ground, a small park with bright flower-beds. Mr Kimberley's idea was to give people interludes of easy, happy times in order to encourage and make possible self-help. In this environment individual talents could thrive and prosper. The club was run in 1929 by boys who had previously vandalised it. The Sub-Warden himself controlled the club's premises – ignoring his own war disability of an amputated leg, he was passionate about providing work and activities which welded body, spirit and mind.

Mr Kimberley invited Vi Brown to an inaugural meeting of a Mother's Club. If all this seems terribly politically incorrect, then firstly, these were different times in a different era of class consciousness, and secondly, political correctness is now rebounding in on itself, imploding at an ever-increasing speed. Lyminster House and gardens became the base for their day's summer outing. This chapter gives a special insight into the atmosphere and events of the day. In 1934 a veritable army of helpers prepared Lyminster for the great fleet of buses which transported the Millwall families. This army was commanded by the formidable Maud Cooper, who was in specific charge of the catering. Mr Asplin, the head gardener and cricket groundsman, laid out the trestle tables which were festooned in a variety of garden flowers. He was helped by his wife in a hundred and one various tasks. What the military might call a 'Special Forces' unit was made up of Cecil, Linda, Polly and Richard Cooper; Dr. Duval the Vicar, stout of heart and figure; Mrs Duval, tiny, slight and indomitable; Mr Hoole, ex-Naval PO and present publican and Mrs Hoole, an ex-Governor of Wormwood Scrubs.

Mineral waters and brown stout refreshed both young and old. Young babies were brought, but not other children – this annual day was for mothers who could forget their cares for a while. After lunch, the buses took the entourage to Littlehampton beach, although the more elderly stayed behind to doze or chat. By 5.00, the seaside throng returned for ham, tongue, tomatoes, strawberries, cakes and gallons of tea. The guests, always courteous, ungreedy and meticulous about collecting their litter, were at the centre of the friendly army of helpers.

A special character was one Mary Croley, a die-hard cockney through and through, a natural comic, a Nellie Wallace clone if ever there was one. Seven years later in 1941, Mary wrote to Vi Brown, remembering in particular the day in 1934 when the sun seemed to shine harder and hotter than on all the rest of their visits. Mary had danced the Highland Fling with Vi Brown, ending up turning somersaults!

Isle of Dogs,
July 1941

…are you troubled with the raids much? The poor old island had a right smash up and lots of our club people have passed on, God rest their souls. We still go to the club and Chapel. Mr Kimberley is very busy these days and he looks rather sad and tired at times. I wish and pray that this lousy war was over, it all seems very wicked to me. Land mines and bombs are dropping all around, houses rock, blown up. I felt me heart come off me hooks. Some sleeps in their shelters, some in the underground, I sleeps in the home on me ground floor. When I see the flares drop I call them the devil's eyes! One day in the near future this poor old world will be at peace again please God. How are you and your family, Mrs Cooper and her children. Polly and Richard will have grown into a lovely boy and girl now. I do so hope you will understand my scribble, but my hand hurts and it is rather crippled up, anyway I hope this will find you as well and happy as time will allow. Cheerio. God bless us all!

Love from Mary Croley.

P. S. I am getting quite an old crow now, but who cares as long as the war ends quick.

Good luck, bye-bye.

Mary had enclosed a bright tartan handkerchief with a Scots piper dancing in one corner to commemorate their Scottish dancing in 1934. She exchanged letters with Vi Brown up until 1951.

These events are a small window into the world of the 1930s, not a world where the rich always ignored the poor, although the majority of the affluent did so. The Browns were idealists. Real poverty might now be a thing of the past, but we have retreated into our homes, cut off from the rest of society. A society where the nuclear family is a growing rarity, let alone the extended family.

As a follow up to the Women's day out at Lyminster, cricket matches were played between The House XI and a side from Docklands Settlement No. 2 are clearly recorded. The Lyminster score book records a draw between the two sides in 1939.

Dockland Settlement No. 2			**Lyminster House XI**		
Coats		93	J. Turner		34
Waterson		15	T. Tomset		0
Woodhall		5	J. F. Barrett		71
Durham		41	P. Horsford		6
Jennings		13	H. A. Craxton		4
Walters		2	I. Craxton	N. O.	15
Hames.	n. o	0	J. Rich		3
Taylor			U. Baliol-Scott	N. O.	5
McCarthy			P. Squires		
Sprackling			J. MacDonald		
Sullivan			C.C. Cooper		
Total	171 for 6 declared		**Total**	151 for 6	

Anthony Craxton 3–24   Coats 2–24
Match drawn.

Ursel Baliol-Scott was a stalwart of the Lyminster House side and a loyal Trifler. His brother was later Under-Secretary to the Minister of Supply, Leslie Burgin.

Chapter 9

1934 – 'Haven't declared...they have!'

Havant cricket club were regular opponents of the Triflers in the 30s. The 1934 saw a great club game, with a total of 521 runs scored in an afternoon. It reflects the importance of declaring at the correct time, in order to create the classic game.

August 25th, 1934

Havant CC			The Triflers CC		
J.P. Parker		134	F.E. Pagan		50
G.W.S. Brown		73	J.C. Bune		28
S.H. Palmer		13	J. Alderson		72
Rev. G.L.O. Jessop		46	J.F. Carson		33
F. Brundrett		5	J.S. Brown		11
H.G. Boswell		1	R.E. Symes-Thompson		1
J.P. Blake	D.N.B.		J.P. Rayne		1
T.L. Turney	D.N.B.		H. G. Crabtree		10
R.J. Gates	D.N.B.		A. C-Johnson	N. O.	3
A. Noble	D.N.B.		J.O.H. Powell-Jones	N. O.	1
F. Baker	D.N.B.		J.E. Rich	D.N.B.	
Total declared	278 for 5 wickets		**Total**	243 for 8 wickets	

A. C-Johnson 5–100   H. G. Boswell 3–57

Havant had scored their runs off only 45 overs. Alan Campbell-Johnson's patient slow left arm bowling was rewarded with five wickets. J. P Parker's superb 134 was

84

typical of the man who played many times for Hampshire as an amateur. The Rev. G. L. O. Jessop hit nine fours in his innings of 46, before being caught by John Brown off the bowling of Alan Campbell-Johnson. It was always a battle between Jessop and Campbell-Johnson in the 30s. Would Jessop be caught on the boundary, beaten in the flight by the wily slow left armer? Or would Campbell-Johnson be hit over the top for a series of boundaries. Slow bowlers seemed more content to buy their wickets in those days. Many club cricketers who today predominantly play in leagues would struggle to comprehend the ethos and morality involved with an all day declaration game. The Havant fixture produced the epitome of the classic match. The Triflers, batting second, had a good go at getting the runs, before they held on for a well earned draw.

Two days later on August 27th, 1934, the Triflers played Bognor Regis CC. Guesting for the Triflers that day was the great Sussex batsman Hugh Bartlett, who only just missed out on an England cap, being selected the once on a full MCC tour. True to form, he hit 144 not out, putting on 195 runs with opener Francis Pagan, in a total of 279 for 3 wickets declared. Bognor just held on for a draw, being 150 for 9 at stumps.

The second classic game of the Triflers Cricket Week of August 1934, was the match against Steyning, C. J. 'Juggy' Holden's 151 not out dominating their total of 251 for 7 wickets declared. The Triflers finished the day on 249 for 6 wickets, a mere two runs short of their target. John Bune (58), John Alderson (78) and Robin Edgar (80) scored the bulk of the runs. It is sad to note that all four batsmen who played so well that day met early deaths. Robin Edgar died of yellow fever whilst working in Nigeria for H M Colonial Service Overseas. 'Juggy' Holden, John Bune and John Alderson were killed in the war.

The people foresaw another World War in 1934. The

Germans had voted to give Hitler dictatorial powers on August 19th. On November 28th, Winston Churchill spoke to the House, warning them of the growing threat of German air strength, but these were only distant rumblings. Churchill's worries were supported by a government report which stated that Hitler was our greatest potential enemy. A programme of rearmourment was needed to in order to have an expeditionary force ready to deal with any emergencies. Just exactly how much investment would be placed in the armed forces became the centre of acrimonious parliamentary debates over the proceeding years. Cricket and cream teas were a far more appealing thought.

Chapter 10

1935 – Spectators: the people of Lyminster

Triflers at the Lyminster cricket week.

In 1935 Hitler internally consolidated the Nazi regime in Germany, concentrating on squashing any opposition to the Nazi party. He demanded complete devotion from all Germans as he atomised society, cutting off people from their families, their first loyalty being to the Fuhrer and the

Third Reich. The Nuremberg Laws were followed by the law which gave Nazis ground for divorce if their spouses were non-believers. Hitler did not threaten the Versailles Peace Treaty until the following year. The major threat to peace in 1935 came when Mussolini invaded Ethiopia, thereby bullying a weak and vulnerable country.

1935 Polly Cooper watching the cricket

John Brown had left Trinity College, Cambridge, in June 1934, with a Class II(i) in his English Tripos. The day after graduating, he married Nesta Clement-Jones, daughter of the shipbuilder Sir Clement-Jones. Nesta later became 'Wardrobe Mistress of the Royal Ballet' at Covent Garden. John, the founder of the Triflers' Cricket Club, was appointed as an English Master at the Edinburgh Academy and had started in September 1934. From here he was able to network and bring many Scottish Triflers to Sussex as well as promote the first Scottish Tour in 1936.

In June 1935, Maud Cooper concluded a long list of

groceries and provisions over the telephone with the rider ...and ONE child's chamber, PREFERABLY blue!

John Brown and Nesta Clement-Jones' Wedding.

John Brown's wedding. From the left, Meg Burgin, Jill Burgin, Leslie Burgin MP, Diana Burgin, Frank Woodruff.

This signified the birth of John and Nesta Brown's son Andrew who later won his Full Colours at Sherborne School and played for the Royal Navy in the 1950s, thereby continuing the tradition of the game in the family.

Alongside the white sight screen on the front limits of Lyminster House and top of the ha-ha, was the perfect place for watching cricket. Either in the sun or under the shade of lime trees during days that scorched, a striking view of Arundel Castle to the north rounded off the idyllic setting. Besides spare Triflers, there were their fiancees, wives or even children, including young Andrew Brown, grandson of Vi and CNB, clapping when others clapped, or careering about on a tiny tricycle for relief – there were some remarkable regulars.

Auntie Maud Cooper

Auntie Maud Cooper.

The amply bosomed Auntie Maud was Vi Brown's first cousin and was made 'Quartermaster-General' to the Browns, being responsible for organising a collection of servants and organising domestic affairs. The word 'affairs' is rather unfortunate as Maud had hitherto led a most unCooper-like existence, straying away from orthodox Methodist morals! She had been 'housekeeper' to one Mr Clutsum, or 'Clutty', as he was known by Maud. This always irked Vi Brown who regarded this as looking back through rose-tinted spectacles. G.H. Clutsum was an Australian composer who modified the broadway hit musical "Blossom Time" for audiences and retitled it "Lilac Time". It ran for 626 continuous performances at the Lyric Theatre on Shaftesbury Avenue.

Vi Brown euphemistically 'rescued' Maud from the perceived evils of this arrangement! If the truth be known, 'Clutty' lived with Maud when it suited him, since he was already married! Vi's outrage was tempered by her action in inviting Maud to work at Lyminster. There was a lot more to Auntie Maud than met the eye. She was a gifted artist and photographer, her work remaining in the family to the present day. During the war when Vi Brown opened Lyminster House to all the Armed Forces, teetotal Tea Dances were held in the Billiards Room. Maud laced the fruit cup with brandy and cider. The Cameron Highlanders of Ottawa were mightily impressed!

Osborne the butler and Connie the maid

The whole of Maud's staff would come out to watch the cricket matches, including Osborne, the butler, and Connie, one of the maids. As Mr and Mrs Osborne, they would later come back and visit the house shortly after Maj.-Gen. Ronnie Buckland and his wife Judith bought the western half of the house in 1977. They were looking for the potting shed where they once canoodled, away from the moral gaze of Vi Brown. Osborne once gave Connie a pair of frilly knickers, which she refused to accept, saying that she would only receive such items from the man she would marry! Osborne was later successful in his offer of underwear and they lived happily ever after. There was also Annie the cook who had faithfully moved down from St John's Wood with the Browns. Her cricket teas, laid out in front of the visitors' pavilion, were legendary. Teatime at cricket matches is an English ritual, and a variety of mini-feasts would be unfurled as spectators as well the players took the most traditional of breaks, much loved by the English. Tartan rugs and wickerwork picnic baskets lined the boundary as cricket watchers overdosed on cucumber sandwiches and Victoria sponge.

Linda Cooper

My grandmother was an avid cricket watcher. She was a proud Australian who knew the finer points of the game and followed the sport until her death at the age of 86 at Combe St Nicholas near Chard, Somerset. My grandmother knew her cricket backwards! Her nephew, Trevor Steer, captain of Northern Victoria, would later toss the coin with one Sir Garfield Sobers for a limited overs game during the Windies 65–66 tour. Trevor also was 'Ruckman' and vice-captain of the Collingwood Australian Rules side during their golden era of the mid- to late-50s, when Grand Finals would be played in front of crowds exceeding 120,000 at the Melbourne Cricket Ground. She never lost her love for the game, listening to commentaries on the Ashes on the radio late into the night and following my more modest exploits for North Perrott CC and Wadham School Staff XIs in Somerset of the 1970s and 80s.

Living in the shadow of the Browns and the extended Cooper family was not easy for one who was given the 'poor little Australian' tag, but Gran Cooper ran Lyminster Farm superbly well after my grandfather rejoined the Army in 1941. Gran Cooper was courageous, tactful and warm-hearted. I don't know how many folk in the family would have coped with uprooting their home and moving across the other side of the globe.

The village vicar

One of the regular spectators was Dr. Duval, the Vicar of Lyminster, generally with Christopher, his outsized Aberdeen, firmly at rest beneath his chair. This was the only dog allowed by the formidable Vi Brown to have exclusive tenure at the ground or in the gardens! Owing to his long life at the vicarage this dog was known as Christopher Duval – this added weight to his own self-assurance. Visiting Cooper cousins had to leave their dogs to watch proceedings from an upstairs window in the house! Christopher ruled the roost over the whole of Church Lane as well as the glebe!

Metaphorically speaking, the Vicar of the Saxon Church at Lyminster made a large impression with the young Polly Cooper:

He was a choleric man who intrigued my brother Richard and me because he wore a little mortar board hat with a lovely black tassel that bobbed up and down as he bustled past our cottage on the way to Matins. We were very impressed because we had to call him Dr. Duval and it took some time to latch on to the fact that he was a Doctor of Divinity and not a proper doctor. Being 'Divine', or so we thought, we felt he shouldn't be so fat, but it was a well known fact that 'Steeny' was very fond of his tucker and would often fall asleep at Aunt Vi Brown's after one of Annie the cook's wonderful meals! He also had a very short temper and that scared brother Richard and me.

Dr. and Mrs Duval were childless, but Mrs Duval, daughter of parents who were Missionaries to India, made a great fuss of all the local children and that made us very fond of her. The tiny Mrs Duval had a wonderful dressing up box full of saris and exotic clothes from India. The best of all was her wedding dress, it was so small that I reckon it fitted me perfectly from about the age of seven!

My Mum used to go down to the local sewing circle to help make dresses for the local Zenana Mission. These simple frocks were meant to cover up the native women and so help to bring them to righteousness and Christianity. However, Mrs Duval didn't think it suitable for Mum to join the local sewing bee as she was connected to the land-owning classes of Lyminster! She was a hopeless seamstress anyway so she wasn't too bothered. I think her transgression of the class barriers was forgiven because after all, she was only a colonial who didn't understand the nuances of English country life.

Dr. Duval did have one good point. He would take us to church and show us an ancient tomb fixed to the wall near the font and tell us the story of the Knight whose gravestone it was:

'A long time ago there had been a dragon who lived in the Knucker Hole. This was a bottomless circular pond just off the track that led to Lyminster Church over the fields to Arundel Castle. This dragon had been terrifying the local inhabitants, coming out of the pond and gobbling up the children and cattle.

'After a lot of worrying the Knight volunteered to do away with the menace. He had a plan. Realising how greedy the dragon was, he knew it wouldn't resist his mother's cake which the Knight himself could not bear. It was so heavy and indigestible! The Knight asked his mother to bake the biggest cake she had ever made. She was happy to oblige being very proud of her own cooking. When the huge and heavy cake was ready, it was hauled on to a cart, and the horse staggered down the lane to the Knucker Hole. Here the Knight backed the cart up to the hole and was just about to unharness the cart when the whole thing became unbalanced and cake and cart and horse shot up into the air, flipping over backwards into the pond. Up came the dragon from the bottom of the bottomless pool and swallowed the whole caboodle in one go. It was too much and too heavy and the dragon sank into the Knucker Hole and was never seen again!'

We thought it interesting that Dr. Duval himself was very partial to fruit cake, but never had the nerve to tell him to keep away from the Knucker Hole himself!

"Legends of Lyminster". Miss Duke and Mrs King with the mini Coopers. Abbotsford Gardens, 1934

Mrs King, Mrs Fergusson and Miss Duke

Mrs King was a slight, white-haired lady who came to watch *every* ball bowled and sat apart or only with genuine lovers of the game. Mrs Fergusson, who lived at another Georgian mansion in the village, sometimes accompanied Mrs King. Mrs Fergusson actually lived with a Mr Wright, who was officially the housekeeper. Apparently this was not the case!

Miss Duke came from a long line of Lyminster Dukes. She was still an energetic lady, into her 80s by the time the final home Triflers' fixture was played. She bequeathed 'Duke's Field' to the village, stating that it must never be built on. It still stands in Lyminster today as a green epitaph to a fine Englishwoman. Her family tomb lies close to the main door of Lyminster Church.

Mr and Mrs Asplin

Mr Asplin, the cricket groundsman, grew all the vegetables for the Browns at Lyminster House. His state-of-the-art greenhouses and walled garden were perfect for this. The strawberries were particularly popular with the visiting teams! Asplin was also allowed to sell commercially extra produce grown by himself. The Browns were fair employees, who encouraged all their staff. Asplin's right to become an independent grower was almost an example of an early 'worker share' system. In 1939 there were plans to grow tropical fruit, especially apricots, in a series of hothouses. War stopped this grandiose scheme. CNB and Vi remained absolutely fair to their staff for the rest of their days, always providing proper accommodation with modern amenities.

Mr Asplin was assisted by Bill Town, the house-cum-garden boy. Bill later drowned on HMS Mohawk. All seven Town brothers had joined the Royal Navy, a very fine family of young men well respected by Vi Brown.

Mr Lane

At the northern end of the cricket ground, a sight screen was made by Mr Lane, the Brown's handyman and carpenter. He had been apprenticed in early days to a cabinet maker, and had been a house-painter and policeman too, never losing his policeman's rhythm and measured gait. His health suffered permanently as a legacy of shrapnel still in his lung from World War One. Mr Lane's work was always immaculate and the finished sight screen stood on top of the ha-ha wall shutting out the glint of the windows in the house behind. It is from here that he normally watched the cricket.

Tip and run cricket players during the tea break at Lyminster House. Linda Cooper and Dr. Duval back row, far left.
Richard and Polly Cooper and their cousins.

Young Polly Cooper (13) and brother Richard Cooper (10) would occasionally be joined by visiting cousins such as Tony, Mary and Jean-Steph Woodruff. Tony joined the Indian Army during the war, and later become an actor. His best part was that of the Doctor in *Some Mothers Do 'Av 'Em* when Betty, Frank's wife was expecting a baby. Michael Crawford recounted on a Radio 4 interview in 1999 that Tony had to seek divine help from a vicar the night before the filming of the hospital scene, as he could not help but burst into hysteric laughter at Frank's exploits!

The Burgin cousins stayed in their parents' caravan under the shade of the lime trees near the boundary. Meg Burgin, married to Bernard Budd, later a High Court Judge specialising in Patent Designs, would be joined by her younger sisters, Jill and Jennifer. Jill Burgin married a doctor, Donald Craig. Jennifer, who died in 1999, married a lawyer, Sir Max Harries Williams, later Chairman of the Law Society and Senior Partner at Clifford Chance. Diana Burgin married John Alderson in 1939.

1935: Coopers, Browns and Woodruffs at Lyminster house.

The Floods

John and Yeoma Flood were the brother and sister of Triflers' wicket-keeper Bobby Flood, later a Brigadier in the British Army. The Floods' father was a vicar in Littlehampton. Richard Cooper and John would take breaks from the cricket and find adventure driving a horse-drawn rake with Harold Endersby, gathering hay into large bundles before it was transferred to the donkey cart and stacked onto huge ricks. Sheaves of wheat were stacked into stooks in time-honoured fashion – an enduring rural image of pre-war Sussex.. It was in these fields where the seeds of my father's later career in farming were sown. John Flood was my parents' best man in 1951.

Uncle Syddie Cooper

It always amused young Polly Cooper when Uncle Syddie, Maud's brother, came to visit Lyminster from Worthing. Dressed in two-tone brogues with a 'Norf London' accent to match, he did not quite fit in with the image of Lyminster! Rumour had it that, evil of all evils, Syddie was a bookmaker! This subject was avoided by Vi – her idealism did get muddled on occasions. The Cooper family was a large extended mass and Lyminster became the centre of many of its summer activities in the 1930s: gatherings of Browns, Woodruffs, Burgins and Coopers would watch the cricket or gather for informal parties.

The farmworkers

Harold Endersby very often umpired, particularly when the Lyminster House XI played. He lived in a bothy above the Coach House, although he always went home to his mother's for meals. Harold was in charge of the donkey and donkey cart, used for a thousand and one farmyard jobs, including taking in the harvest in the summer. During the war, the donkey was later nicknamed 'Yevoshenko' after the famous Russian General, because the animal was 'stubborn in retreat!'

Mr Mills was a keen watcher of games. He was also the expertly skilled haystack builder, and although he was getting rather long in the tooth, he refused to give in to either old age or rheumatics. Mills loved to tell Polly and

Richard Cooper that he had once been over six feet tall and that he had shrunk! This was due, in fact, to staggering home from the Six Bells in Lyminster. Mills had to jump a wide ditch with his drinking pals. Mills's mates played the trick of shining the guiding torch in the middle of the murky waters. Mills landed with a 'plop' into the stagnant mire! Bob Lane, the carpenter, suffered from the effects of wounds received in the First World War, but this never affected his superb woodworking skills.

Bill Blessed was the immaculately dressed senior herdsman. The standard attire was a white chef's style hat, starched collar and tie. He took charge of the apprentice cowmen, Tom Tomsett and later George Carmen, and they would all join the spectators at matches after milking. Tom was a keen cricketer himself and played in many matches for my grandfather's Lyminster House XI.

The Sissons

Charles Jasper Sisson was a Professor of Shakespearean Literature and had worked in Universities in India, Egypt and France. His wife Vera and two daughters, Daphne and Rosemary, together with the family dog, Beau, were watchers of the willow at Lyminster, relaxing in the tranquil setting, and admiring the view of Arundel Castle through the lime trees. Rosemary's writing career would later take her to Hollywood, working on Walt Disney films.

Chapter 11

Edmund Symes-Thompson – cavalier cricketer!

The cricket at Lyminster went from strength to strength as the Triflers and their opposition teams got to know each other from one year to the next. The arrival of Edmund Symes-Thompson in the Triflers set-up was a great boost to the Lyminster scene, both on and off the cricket field. He came from four generations of medical practitioners. His grandfather had been professor of medicine and consultant at King's College Hospital, London. His father was Consulting Physician to the Royal Chest Hospital, London. Young Symes-Thompson, a Cambridge University medical student and an ex-Radleian, was a jovial fountain of very good stories, and his casual corpulence masked a good cricketer and a thoughtful man. Edmund had the gift of being able to keep a company of varying outlooks and ages helpless with laughter while he told a funny story. A real depth of humanity though lay beneath this comic exterior.

Edmund played his cricket for the pure love of the game, being an excellent all-rounder. Solid of build from an early age, he carried the sort of weight that matched his rosy red cheeks and twinkling brown eyes. Hitting boundaries always had a higher priority than scampering short singles! On August 22nd, 1935 he hit 12 fours whilst compiling the third ever century scored by a Trifler. His 117 not out resulted in a victory of 84 runs against old rivals Steyning.

A letter from Edmund to Auntie Vi in the war illuminates his larger than life character and gentle wit, and is also a cameo of the archetypal English cricketer. Absolutely wonderful! The following letter is taken from Vi's book *The Silver Cord*.

Finmere House
(Buckingham)
as from April 14th, '41 St Luke's Hospital, Chelsea.

My dear Mrs Brown,
                Just a line out of the blue to send you my best wishes at the beginning of cricket season 1941. I haven't oiled my bat, and I haven't cleaned my boots, but today I put on my MCC tie in honour of the opening of the Spring Offensive against the armies of General Half-Volley and Major-General Longhop.

How are you all at Lyminster and what is the news from Edinburgh and the Triflers?

Today I return to town again for another six months, which will, I imagine, be rather more disturbing than before; however, six or seven breakfasts in bed down here have revived me. – I felt as tired as after our big Scottish drive – do you remember? When I came down here it felt like 'two May weeks of fatigue', but now I am revived by digging potatoes.

I hope Mr Brown is well and not overworking and that you have finished with your illness. Chelsea has been quiet for the last few weeks, but we are so short of staff and drugs at the moment that it makes things a bit difficult.

Please give my love to all at Lyminster.

Yours ever,
Edmund.

Very shortly after this letter was written, Edmund was killed – on Sunday, May 11th, 1941, almost at the end of London's first long ordeal. According to Auntie Vi, Edmund was under the path of a direct hit on St Luke's Hospital, Chelsea, while he was carrying out a blood transfusion. Whilst researching this book, I tracked down Edmund's family after a chance report in the *Guardian* concerning his nephew, the Rev. Symes-Thompson, and a Millennium bells campaign in his parish. The Symes-Thompson family had incredibly just started enquiries into Edmund's life as a prelude to a family reunion in the year 2000. It is very probable that young Edmund was in bed with a nurse at the time of his death. From my telephone conversations it became apparent that Edmund was what was euphemistically termed in those days as something of a 'Ladies Man'. I will leave the story of Edmund here, but suffice it to say there was more to the young man that met the eye. Well, certainly from the puritanical outlook of Auntie Vi!

Lord Rodney Smith

Rodney Smith, a famous Trifler, brought a team of medical students down from London to play at Lyminster on August 25th, 1935. Smith was training at St Thomas's Hospital under the formidable senior surgeon, Philip Mitchiner, an eccentric crew-cropped man of outstanding surgical ability and forthright views, which did not prevent him from being awarded the CB in 1944 and the CBE in 1953. He represented the Surrey 2nd XI team and could have also made a career as a professional violinist. Whilst training at St Thomas's Medical School he was both William Tite and Peacock scholar and he won the Grainger Prize for research. When the Second World War broke out, he was just setting out in his career as a surgeon, specialising in the bile and pancreas.

His brilliant medical career reached a peak when he became President of the Royal College of Surgeons from 1973 to 1975. Smith was elected President of the British Medical Association for 1981, but a bad stroke meant that he had to stand down.

His obituary in Westminster School's *Elizabethan* magazine is an interesting one as it reflects a rather ruthless and detached figure. A great raconteur and Cockney mimic, he sought only a few close friends. A snippet from the *Elizabethan* reflects the sterner side of his character:

> ...a lack of understanding of lesser mortals. As a surgeon he was the supreme technician with some interest in diagnosis but less in the problems of clinical care.

The Triflers won the match against E. R. Smith's XI by 59 runs, Smith's 27 being top score in a total of 86. Knighted in 1972, Rodney Smith took his seat in the House of Lords in 1978. He died in 1998.

The next day the Triflers travelled to play against Bognor, who arguably fielded the strongest side ever to face them in the 1930s. The opposition was full of famous men of pre-war Sussex cricket. Hugh Bartlett, F. W. Gilligan and S. C. Griffith all contributed to a Bognor victory of 109 runs. Rodney Smith and Francis Pagan had earlier put on 93 runs for the first wicket, but the remaining nine wickets totalled only 48 runs.

August 27th, 1935

Bognor Regis CC			The Triflers' CC		
M.N. Ireland		73	E.R. Smith		44
H.T. Bartlett		52	F.E. Pagan		48
P.H. Brewerton		34	R.W. Edgar		5
F.W. Gilligan		43	J. Alderson		14
S.C. Griffith	N. O.	25	R.E. Symes-Thompson		0
N.E. Carter	D.N.B.		P.W. Cocks		2
J.C.L. Sharman	D.N.B.		J.S. Brown		2
B. Darewski	D.N.B.		U. Baliol-Scott		2
Col. A.C. Byrne	D.N.B.		W.R.S. Doll		12
N. Darewski	D.N.B.		J.E. Rich	N. O.	3
C.B. French	D.N.B.		W.E. Heard		0
Total	248 for 4 wickets declared		Total	139 all out	

P.W. Cocks 2–48 C.B. French 5–46   B. Darewski 4–41

Bognor Regis won by 109 runs

'Billy' Griffith and Hugh Bartlett

S. C. 'Billy' Griffith and Hugh Tryon Bartlett remained life-long friends, brought together by their love of Sussex cricket and their great skill in playing the game. Griffith played for Sussex throughout the 30s, but it was not until after the war that he was picked for his country, going on the MCC tour of the West Indies. He made 140 in 6 hours at the crease in the second test, stating afterwards that he was too scared to return to the pavilion and face Jack Robertson after running him out! During the war, Griffith was Second in Command to Major-General M. G. 'Windy' Gale, piloting the glider which took Gale to D-Day. He later took part in the landings at Arnhem where he was awarded the DFC.

'Billy' Griffith became Secretary of the MCC in 1961. He died in a nursing home at Felpham, Sussex, in 1978, aged 78. Sadly, it was Maj.-Gen. Gale's sister who inadvertently set fire to her bedroom in Hampton Court, thereby starting the tragic fire of 1987.

Hugh Bartlett died ten years later, while watching his beloved Sussex during a Sunday League game in June 1988. He was probably the hardest-hitting left-handed batsman of his era, although not quite as stylish as the great Frank Woolley. Bartlett scored over 2000 runs for Cambridge in one season before joining Sussex. In 1937, he was selected for the MCC tour to South Africa, but never played in a test. Like Griffith, he was awarded the DFC during the war. In 1947, Bartlett was appointed captain of Sussex.

Sir Richard Doll: cancer specialist

The 1935 season ended with two matches against Havant CC. Both games were low scoring affairs with Havant winning the first by 3 wickets, Triflers' wicket-keeper Richard Doll top scoring with 40. John Blake secured a close victory for Havant. In the return fixture on September 7th, John Alderson's typically dashing innings of 54 not out won the match for the Triflers. Francis Pagan took the crucial wicket of Havant's F. Bundrett who had scored 71, and cleaned up the tail taking 3–6 with his slow bowling.

**Sir Richard Doll and John Brown take
the field at Lyminster , 1935.**

Sir Richard Doll applied for a mathematics Scholarship at Cambridge University on leaving Westminster School in 1931. All was going well until three pints of strong ale the night before resulted in a poor examination paper the day after!!! This set Sir Richard on a medical career at St. Thomas's Hospital in London. His passion for social justice saw him attend the Jarrow Marchers on their famous crusade. His interest in socialism took him to Russia and his medical studies saw him study in Germany where the evils of Nazism was seen at first hand. Sir Richards questioning of the obnoxious creed had him labelled as a "Jew" during his time in Germany. Aunty Vi remembers him pacing up and down the ha-ha in the 30's, pondering on whether to join the fight against Fascism during the Spanish Civil war. Richard and his brother Christopher lived at Slinfold, playing for the club before they both joined the Triflers. Christopher Doll was a Spitfire pilot during the war and was decorated many times; he was married to Josephine Douglas of BBC *Family Forces Favourites* fame. Later, in 1967, Richard would be the first person to prove a link between smoking and cancer. Richard Doll had been working on the project for over 20 years. In fact, he commented about it to Grandpa Cooper in 1947 during a visit to see the Browns and Coopers after their move to Wayford, near Crewkerne, a year earlier. My grandfather last saw Richard Doll in 1964 when my grandmother was meeting her sister Australian Elizabeth Lee in London. Elizabeth had travelled over from Australia with Judy Tegart and her manager. Tegart, later Judy Dalton, became the darling of the Wimbledon Centre Court crowds in the late 60s and early 70s.

Richard Doll received the OBE in 1956 and was knighted in 1971. President of the Royal College of Physicians, the honour bestowed on him by the *Guardian* in 1998 as one of the twentieth century's most influential men and women was based on the premise that his work had the greatest effect on world health. Sir Richard Doll had literally changed man's perception of the cigarette overnight. He served as the Treasurer of the Triflers from 1932 to 1939, and match manager on many occasions.

Chapter 12

1936 – The Berlin Olympics, the Spanish Civil War, the first Triflers' tour to Scotland

On March 29th, 1936, the Nazi Party won 99 per cent of the total votes cast in the German elections. It gave them the confidence and strident arrogance to march into the Rhineland, thus breaking a key point of the 1919 Versailles Treaty. The League of Nations were outraged, but they did nothing to stop Hitler's relentless destruction of the treaty all Germans detested. The previous year had seen Neville Chamberlain, in his position of Chancellor of the Exchequer, persuade the Prime Minister Stanley Baldwin to spend £1500 million on our armed forces. The problem was that too much spending would plunge Britain back into deep recession. The army, though, was in no position to fight a modern war. The Chiefs of Staff endorsed appeasement when they accepted this reality. In Parliament, it was only Churchill who consistently stated that we were underestimating the speed of Germany's rearmourment. Appeasement was being balanced with controlled rearmourment: it was a two-pronged strategy.

On August 1st, 1936 Adolf Hitler opened the Berlin Olympic Games, an event which he pathetically thought would prove Aryan supremacy over the rest of the world.

Thankfully, the black American sprinter and long jumper Jesse Owens destroyed Hitler's racist hopes, winning four Gold medals. Hitler stormed out of the stadium, refusing to present the medals to Owens. 'The Olympics,' Owen later said in Cliff Morgan's all-time favourite sporting interview, 'were a chance to break bread with the rest of the world.'

The Browns and the 1936 Olympics

Whilst Hitler was choking on these metaphorical crusts of Olympic conciliation, great-aunt Vi Brown and her husband CNB followed the Games from Lyminster House with special interest. CNB's two nephews and niece – Godfrey, Ralph and Audrey Brown – had been selected for the Great Britain Athletics squad. This was a unique triumvirate in British Olympic history, which was destroyed when Ralph had to pull out with a hamstring injury. Godfrey Brown, later headmaster of Worcester Royal Grammar School, won a Silver medal in the individual 400 metres race and a Gold medal in the 4 x 400 metres relay.

All the Browns except for Godfrey had been educated at the Methodist foundation, Kingswood School, Bath. Godfrey attended Warwick School, as he was staying with an elderly aunt and uncle when his mother and father went to work as Methodist missionaries in India. CNB had loved Kingswood and all it stood for, and it was where his nonconformist benevolent beliefs took root. His father had also been a poor Methodist missionary in India. Godfrey and Ralph's other brother, Leonard, was the only nephew who was a regular Trifler, and later became Director of Education in Yorkshire. Ralph became a High Court judge, and was knighted in 1970. As Kingswood School's oldest and most prominent pupil, he opened the extension to Middle House in 1992. Today my son Gareth, the youngest living Cooper male from the original nine Finchley Coopers of Vi Brown and Cecil Cooper's family, attends the school. The first member of the 25 Coopers, Coleys, Browns, Budds and Scotts (to attend Kingswood School) who formed the extended family, was one George Cooper who became Liberal MP for Bermondsey in the late 1890's.

Freddie 'Thunderbum' Whitelaw and Dick Evers

Cricket at Lyminster was flourishing: aunt Vi Brown arrived home from her American holiday to Virginia and South Carolina just in time to see the ground in perfect shape for the new season. The two major developments were the first of four Triflers' tours to Scotland, and the first appearance of the Sussex Club and Ground XI on the fixture list at Lyminster. John Brown co-opted several players from Scotland into the Triflers' team, including fast bowler Freddie 'Thunderbum' Whitelaw, a lawyer and brilliant all-rounder, Stephen Hutchinson, a Master at Loretto School, and Dick Evers, a Master at Fettes College. Whitelaw, in particular, confounded his English Trifler colleagues with the way in which his huge in-swinging deliveries straightened up wickedly off the seam. A bowler of rare skill! Dick Evers enjoyed his time in the summers of West Sussex so much that he had the good sense to marry the young lady from behind the bar at an Arundel inn! When the war came he took her back to Fettes, where she became the darling of the school and after Dick's death, she married the future headmaster.

The Scottish tour

The first Scottish tour was chaotic, it was an

achievement to get 11 players together after making separate arrangements to travel hundreds of miles north on slow roads. The first touring team comprised CNB, John Alderson, Cecil Cooper, A. Kinloch, J. F. Turner and J. F. B. Barrett who had travelled up from Sussex; Jack Rich and A. Stainsby from Yorkshire; and, rather late, John Brown, B. Stenhouse and W. B. Thorburn from Edinburgh! Godfrey Crabtree travelled all the way from London to play in the last two games, scoring a match-saving 55 not out against Edinburgh Academy. Francis Pagan and Richard Doll travelled from London on the Friday night to play in one match only. Each lasted only three balls! The Triflers were deeply committed to the cause, their name merely a self-mocking jest in the true spirit of English Corinthian tradition. Their dedication to the game was total. The tour was structured around the following fixtures:

Monday	Manderston
Tuesday	Loretto
Wednesday	Edinburgh Academy
Thursday	Berwick
Friday	Scottish Wayfarers (at Peebles or in Edinburgh)
Saturday	Edinburgh Academicals

Manderston was a beautiful private ground, hidden in rhododendron woods, with clumps of dark green shrubs close to the outfield. Loretto's home patch at Musselborough was a wind-swept contrast, with its sandy-soiled bone-hard ground. Raeburn Place and New Field, the Academy grounds, had normal inland turf; Berwick, on a low curving cliff with an arc-like background of sea deceptively near in the glittering light, tempted impossible sixes; and Peebles was green like Manderston, where the Wayfarers match began at 5.30 p.m. so that even in those long northern evenings, whoever lost the toss batted in the gloaming.

The Scottish Tour would grow in stature to provide great cricket, with great names in Scottish cricket pitting their wits against the Triflers. Names such as R. B. Bruce-Lockhart, B. R. and R. Tod, C. M. R. Shiell, D. Weir, C. R. Dunlop, C. J. R. Mair and P. C. Blair. The most famous of these was R. B. Bruce-Lockheart, a leg-spinning all-rounder who had followed his father's footsteps in going to Cambridge. He won both a Blue and a collection of International Rugby caps for Scotland. He was Headmaster of Loretto school between 1960 and 1976.

P. C. Fletcher's XI, Charterhouse School

On August 12th, 1936 the Triflers played Major P. C. Fletcher's XI at Charterhouse School. The Major was a Master at the school. Francis Pagan recollects that Fletcher was

...an old Marlburian himself, he had at his disposal three of his sons who also went to Marlborough as well as a strong contingent of Old Carthusians. He was a great disciplinarian, and insisted that all his matches should begin at 11.00 precisely, not an easy thing for visiting sides coming from all directions. His sanction was to compel any side not ready to take the field to bat first. In earlier years the Triflers had been so heavily defeated, so to strengthen the side we had invited Donald Knight and Claude Taylor to join us.

By 11.00 only three Triflers were on the ground. John Brown and John Alderson, thanks to JSB's Wolsey Hornet sports car, were able to hold the fort while others dribbled in one by one. After a shaky start we were rescued by Donald and Claude, who had been badly held up by traffic out of London, Donald going on to make his glorious knock of 86. We always wondered what would have happened if our captain had insisted on tossing for innings and if successful had put the home side into bat and asked for eight substitutes. We were never brave enough to try!

Donald Knight: Surrey CC and England

Knight was Master i/c of Cricket at Westminster School, the establishment from which the majority of Triflers originated. Donald Knight, a Cambridge Blue as a Freshman in 1914, made two appearances for England against Warwick Armstrong's 1921 Australian side. His best year had been 1919, when he opened the Surrey batting with Jack Hobbs. Knight scored 1,588 runs at an average of 45.37 that season. A year later, in 1920, he was hit on the head while fielding at short leg and perhaps never quite reached the heights of 1919 again. At the age of 43, he returned to first class cricket for 12 matches with Surrey in 1937, scoring 584 runs at 24.37. He was able to pass on his classical style of batting to the hundreds of pupils he coached at Westminster.

Claude Taylor: Oxford University and Leicestershire CC

Claude Taylor also coached at Westminster, he was an Oxford Blue and played for Leicestershire CCC.

'Jack' Russell: Essex and England

The Westminster School groundsman, Charles Albert (Jack) Russell of Essex and England also played the occasional match for the Triflers. Russell scored 140 and 111 in the 5th test against South Africa at Durban on the 1922–23 tour, making him the first English batsman to score two hundreds in the same test match. A tree was planted at the Durban ground in honour of this feat.

Between 1919 and 1930, Jack Russell never failed to score 1,000 runs in a season for Essex. His 2,575 runs in the 1922 season was the highest aggregate in County Cricket that year.

Sussex County Cricket Club at Lyminster House

The highlight of the 1936 home season at Lyminster was the first appearance of the Sussex Club and Ground XI, a powerful amalgam of experienced County players such as Jack Eaton and G. Pearce, being combined with promising youngsters eager to make their way in County Cricket. In the nine matches leading to this game on August 22nd, 1936, the Triflers had won five and lost two, with the match against the Sussex Martlets being abandoned due to rain, a rare occurrence in the 30s it seems!

The Sussex Club and Ground XI match started at 12.00. The Triflers knew they needed to put up a good fight in order to retain the prestigious fixture. The two sides had scored 396 runs by the time umpires J. Elson Jnr. and G. Stannard removed the bails at 7.00 p.m.

August 22nd, 1936

The Triflers' XI			**Sussex Club and Ground XI**		
F.E. Pagan		32	J. Eaton	N.O.	74
R.W. Edgar		41	Greenwood		0
J.H.N. Foster		81	G.G. Pearce		77
J.S. Brown		3	D. Stevens		0
R.E. Symes-Thompson		4	C. Oakes		11
J. Alderson		0	J. Oakes		0
S.T. Hutchison		5	R. Baxter-Phillips	N.O.	11
K.H.L. Cooper		6	H.P. Chaplin	D.N.B.	
W.F.M. Whitelaw	NO.	13	J.C.S. Doll	D.N.B.	
W.R.S. Doll		0	P.H. Cardew	D.N.B.	
W.E. Heard		2	J. Wood	D.N.B.	
Total	216		**Total**	180–5 wkts	

C. Oakes 5–66 W.F.M. Whitelaw 4–33
J. Oakes 3–20

Match Drawn

This was a great performance by the Triflers, the foundations of which were laid by two patient innings: Francis Pagan, 32 in 60 minutes, and Robin Edgar, 41 in 95 minutes. J. H. N. Foster's 81 providing ideal acceleration before a batting collapse was induced by the Oakes brothers. Jack Eaton and G. G. Pearce added 120 runs for the third wicket, with Pearce out for 77 and Eaton ending up on 74 not out. A great day's cricket!

The *Cricketer* magazine for September 3rd, 1936 gave a glowing report of the first fully fledged Triflers' Cricket Week at Lyminster House. Of 8 matches played, 5 had been won, 1 drawn and 2 unfinished. The report reads as follows:

The Triflers had a successful week at Lyminster House. The cricket was remarkable for W. F. M. Whitelaw's fine bowling; he relies on hitting the stumps more frequently than most other bowlers of his pace, but nevertheless was well supported by excellent fielding through the week. The batting was less instrumental in the victories, but W. R. Evers, F. E. Pagan and J. S. Brown scored consistently. Mention of this Cricket Week must not leave unnoticed the gratitude of everybody concerned to Mr C. N. Brown, whose hospitality at Lyminster is undiminished and even increased by the presence of such natural wickets. This is the first full week the club has had on the ground (constructed 1932–1933), and no one was disappointed.

On September 4th, Vi Brown, proudly holding a copy of the magazine, embarked on a Mediterranean cruise with her son John, daughter-in-law Nesta and grandson Andrew. An Italian fascist showed them around Pompeii and was strongly biased by an Axis outlook on the English. The cheerful Sicilians were totally different in spirit, offering fruit and a warmth of spirit which matched that of the sun. Vi found Taormina a beautiful place, staying at the hotel which became the Nazi headquarters, later bombed by the Allies. The journey along the road back to Messina crossed the bridge over the dry watercourse where the Marine Commandos would later show great courage in the war.

Chapter 13

1936 – A Lyminster House Christmas

The build up to Christmas at Lyminster in 1936 was no different to that in many large country homes, but the Browns always made sure that their staff were treated far better their counterparts in traditional establishments.

The Christmas of 1936 was the first where Polly Cooper definitely knew that her father delivered the early morning presents – his cigarette smoke was a give-away! Waking up her younger eight-year-old brother Richard, they busily investigated the contents of their father's golf stockings before carefully replacing all the items back in the same order in which they were taken out. Polly remembers that:

> When morning eventually came we trooped into their room and went through the charade of finding the presents all over again! Downstairs, Dad lit the dining room fire in the red brick fire place. This had two brick hobs on either side where the tea pot and kettle could be left to simmer. Even the mantle shelf and surrounds were of red brick. The front of the fire was made of porridge coloured cast iron.
>
> The Christmas decorations consisted of home made bunting tediously constructed by licking pre-glued lengths of coloured paper and forming chains that were looped from the corners to the central light fitting. The picture above the fireplace was

garlanded with holly as was the picture rail. A bunch of mistletoe was hung from the frame of the door between the dining room and the kitchen. Dad would attempt to catch Mum, but she would push him off with a 'Not now Cecil!'

After breakfast there were more presents in pillow cases. Usually a lovely book, jig saw and pencil case. One year we got a steam engine which had a real boiler and was heated by a tiny meths flame to produce steam. The only drawback was that we only had a straight track and Dad had to hurtle from end to end with a cloth to pick up the hot engine and turn it round for the run back. We were not allowed to work it because of the danger of burns.

A scene which would be echoed all over the country perhaps, but what came after was certainly more unusual for the average boy and girl:

As tension mounted we were washed, brushed and dressed in our best clothes ready to over the road to Aunty Vi's and Uncle Cecil's for Christmas Dinner. By this time Richard was beside himself with excitement and was sick absolutely everywhere! A special place had to laid for him on a little table in the hall where he had 'bread and milk', more digestible than the feast we others sat down to.

The Dining room was decorated with huge banks of poinsettias brought in from the heated conservatory where small grapes had ripened in the Autumn. Bows of holly were tucked round the frames of the seascapes in their dull gold frames.

The Christmas table for those not banished to the hall was decorated with sprigs of holly, the most beautiful fat pale blue crackers from Harrods, gold edged crinkly paper surmounted by a fairy. Inside would be a jewel or a miniature toy and a riddle and a paper hat. There would be two wine glasses in front of each adult and two silver salt cellars up and down the table interspersed with bon-bon dishes with nuts and raisins and crystallised fruits. The place settings on the bare old mahogany table were from the Spode Dinner Set, white with a mottled blue band edged in gold leaf. The piece de resistance was the cornucopia in the centre of the table filled with oranges, apples and grapes topped with most enormous and luscious pineapple. Uncle Cecil would ritually organise a flutter to guess the number of leaves in the crown as they were ceremoniously pulled off as the gargantuan meal staggered to its Victorian close.

But back to the beginning. Sitting down to the table, minus my brother Richard of course, would be Aunty Vi and Uncle Cecil at head and foot, ranked along the sides would be me, my parents and another Uncle and Aunt or two with their assorted children, Aunty Maud and sometimes Dr. and Mrs Duval, all seated on the precious and fragile looking Chippendale chairs. The 'Rev' made them look particularly so!

Dr. Duval led grace and Aunty Maud Cooper would lumber over to the serving table and carve the enormous turkey. Each helping was handed round by Osborne the Butler and two housemaids would follow with tureens of vegetables followed by bread sauce and gravy. Meanwhile, Uncle Cecil had unlocked his private walk-in cupboard and brought out a special Christmas wine. The names of Chablis and Chambertin, Meursalt or Montrachet would be bandied about with a Chateau Neuf du Pape or Nuits St George. Freshly squeezed lemonade stood in crystal jugs for us children.

After second helpings, Aunty Maud would disappear to supervise the flaming of the Christmas pudding and bear it into the dining room herself. Out would come the Madeira and Stilton under its enormous bell jar with the Bath Oliver biscuits. The party would rise. Uncle Cecil would disappear and them return with Corona cigars for the gentlemen and Aunt Vi would lead us to the sitting room for coffee and liqueurs in time for the King's Christmas Broadcast from Sandringham at three o'clock.

It would then be the turn of Osborne, Annie the cook and the housemaids, together with Mr Asplin, the Head Gardener and his wife, to gather in the Servants Hall for their own Christmas feast on the leftovers. The enormous washing up was gathering. The glasses in the butlers pantry, the plates and tureens in the kitchen sink with the saucepans.

The Browns were kind and generous, as well as being eccentric, the odd quote from Shelley was mixed with puritanical Methodism! This was deplored by Dr. Duval who labelled Shelley as 'That Atheist!

But:

…to hope till Hope creates
From its own wreck the thing it contemplates

became a lodestar during the bad days of the war and the family's subsequent traumas of John Brown's divorce.

What about Richard Cooper though, stuck in the hall, comparing his bread and milk with the ongoing feast?!! He would later name the family farm at Woolminstone near Crewkerne 'Lyminster', in celebration and fond remembrance of those idyllic days in Sussex. No lasting harm done there

Cecil Cooper's letter to his mother and sister Brenda in Finchley early in the new year gave a list of young Richard and Polly's presents: these included a model yacht, an Indian wigwam which saw annual service in the garden of 'Nyarrin' for years to come, a policeman's dressing up set, money from Miss Duke and books from Mrs Duval. Miss Duke was a spinster who bequeathed the field which now comprises the village green, insisting that it should never be built on. Cecil Cooper's war record was not only respected by all the extended family, but by local Lyminster folk as well. Cecil Brown gave him a book written by one of the French artists attached to a Despatch Riders' mess in 1914 who made sketches of enemy positions. Cecil also received a book on the latter stages of the war out in Salonica, where he had been in charge of a machine gun company. A short story of his recounts swimming in Lake Doiran, when the Turkish Cavalry came trotting down the road, forcing Cecil and his mates to hide in the reeds until it was safe to move. Oxygen intake was achieved by using the reeds as a Snorkel device.

Chapter 14

1937 – The Stanfords of Slinfold C.C and Bates the Policeman

On May 5th, 1937, Neville Chamberlain became Prime Minister. The opening of the notorious Buchenwald Concentration Camp on August 1st would have gone largely unnoticed in England. Incredibly, there was blanket censorship of the media in order to restrict the amount of policy information communicated regarding Nazi Germany. Perhaps this is where the policy of appeasement was weakest. We treated Germany with kid gloves: if we were going to ignore them re-arming and marching into the Rhineland, then we were certainly not going to challenge them over their appalling treatment of the Jews and other minority groups in their own country. Hitler's next aim was to get his hands on the Sudetenland, an area of Czechoslovakia inhabited by Germans.

Triflers C.C. vs Arundel C.C.
Lyminster House 22nd August, 1937

Back from left; J. A. McDonald, Gordon Crabtree, Rodney Smith (later Lord Smith), Eric Heard (nephew of Cardinal Heard), Bobbie Flood (later Brigadier Flood), Cecil Cooper. Middle row from left; Edmund Symes-Thompson, (Sir) Richard Doll, John Brown, Francis Pagan, W.F.M. "Thunderbum" Whitelaw. Sitting; Jack Rich, John Alderson

22nd August,1937 Triflers' CC v's Arundel CC at Lyminster House.

Cecil Cooper, Triflers' C.C. leaning on bat.

The cricket scene at Lyminster continued to flourish. The Scottish Tour took place between June 14th and 19th. Some great games against both local opposition and touring sides continued to take place. The match against Slinfold CC was always hard and competitive. The Triflers played Slinfold CC on July 10th, 1937, giving the visitors a chance to avenge a narrow defeat by one wicket at the end of May, earlier in the year. Slinfold were a village side with one or two really good bats and a family of all-rounders by the name of Stanford: A. B., W. H., E. B., J., A. J., and H. A., although Vi Brown was never sure as to whether the last two were not one and the same when she shared the scoring duties with a small boy, whom she could not press too closely! This small boy was, in fact, a young Johnnie Johnson who today forms the backbone of the Slinfold club. The Stanfords were all massive men with the physiques of blacksmiths, builders by trade, and some bowled very fast. Stanford senior was a good umpire and the fount of cricket in his family. In this particular match, three of the Stanford family played.

July 10th, 1937

Triflers CC			Slinfold CC		
E. Symes-Thompson		14	J. Stanford		0
R.W. Edgar		26	A. Knight		2
Cap. J.F.B. Barrett		34	F. Burrage		0
R.C. Bates	N.O.	52	R. Wadey		11
H. G. Crabtree	N.O.	33	S. Sheppard		0
W. R. S. Doll			B. Batchelor		0
B. C. Lee			A. Houndsome		0
Hon. F. Rea			H.A. Stanford		5
R. N. Heaton			F. Dinnage	N.O.	9
J. A. Macdonald			J. Covey		1
Total	166 for 3 wickets declared		**Total**	60 all out	

F. Burrage 2–15

R. C. Bates 5–12
J. A. Macdonald 4–29

The Triflers won by 106 runs

One or two Triflers are worthy of note here. The Hon. Findlay Rea, brother of Lord Rea, later organised all the competitions in the *Cricketer* magazine. Neville Heaton worked as a Secretary in various Government Departments, and in 1944 he was the driving force behind 'Rab' Butler's Education Act of that year. Captain Barrett lived near to Lyminster and J. A. Macdonald was a renowned local bowler.

Police Constable Bates

Perhaps the most interesting character was PC Bates, the village policeman. His analysis of 5–12 in the Slinfold game was not unusual, for he was a tremendous fast left-arm over-the-wicket bowler and a fine all-round athlete. In a later match he took all ten wickets to fall, six clean bowled, one caught at mid-on, and three LBW. Ten years later Vi Brown met him, and heard that the ball presented to him that afternoon still graced his mantelpiece as a cherished trophy, forbidden for use to his son even in the days when balls were hard to come by.

Auntie Vi Brown had been determined to get PC Bates on the annual Triflers' Tour to Scotland in 1937. In pushing Bates's case, she would be breaking the social conventions of the 30s, for a so-called humble Police Constable in reality would not normally be selected for an elitist team. Such rules lay mainly unwritten. Vi Brown did not give a jot about such restrictions and would have thrived on challenging such narrow-mindedness. The problem lay with the Police authorities, not the Triflers, who were only too pleased to see this outstanding player have the chance to compete against the cream of Scotland's cricketers, the teams packed full of Scottish internationals.

Vi sent a letter to the Chief Constable in Chichester requesting an appointment with him. She never understood why her request was turned down, it was a chance in a lifetime for a young cricketer. Perhaps it was a case of inverted snobbery in action, the Chief Constable not taking too kindly to a person of Vi's social standing turning up in sand shoes. Maybe assertive women politically to the left did not go down too well in the England of the 1930s. This was a lady who during the run-up to the 1950 General Election drove her Daimler through the country lanes of Wayford near Crewkerne with a 'Vote Labour' sticker in the rear window! Bates was bitterly disappointed to have the request turned down. He said that every policeman he knew in Sussex would have covered for him. On meeting the Chief Constable at a later social function, Vi Brown greeted him accordingly:

The last time we met…I tried to steal one of your policemen!

He was not at all amused, and tried to ignore the ramifications of the comment. Vi Brown was not one to court popularity though, she thrived on such measured egalitarianism.

Her passion for gardening was immense. After the move from Sussex to Somerset in 1946, Vi Brown became the force behind the first Clapton Flower Show, near Crewkerne, in 1949, a venture which put much colour into a monochrome post-war world. The Lyminster Cup is still presented at the show to this day. In the early 50s, Vi asked her nephew Richard Cooper if his wife Margaret would like to do the flowers for the Clapton Flower Show. Margaret replied that she wouldn't, and her husband had to explain that when Vi asked if something could be done in the family, one didn't enter into negotiations! No lasting damage was done as the Coopers took away the prizes!

Many weekend escapist sides from London played matches at Lyminster including the Refreshers – made up from London Barristers, the Gargoyles, Middlesex Nomads and the Westminster Ramblers, also connected to Westminster School like the Triflers. An untypically low scoring match, for Lyminster was a good batting track, ended in a very tight finish against the Ramblers on 13th August.

August 13th, 1937

The Triflers' CC			**Westminster Ramblers CC**		
F.E. Pagan		11	Wildish		2
Capt. J.F.B. Barrett RN		14	Carmichael		10
C.C. Cooper		11	Symons		53
J.S. Brown		9	Asser		4
G.R. Flood		18	Corie		19
J.H. Veneker		1	Stocker		9
W.F.M. Whitelaw	N.O.	26	Binyon	N.O.	6
H.G. Crabtree		3	Patterson		2
T. Tomsett		8	F. Sludt		0
J.A. Macdonald	D.N.B		W. Sludt	D.N.B	
Dr. R. Barrett	N.O.	16	Heard	N.O.	0
Total	122 for 8 wickets declared		**Total**		116 for 8 wickets

E. Heard 3–39 J. A. Macdonald 5–40
W.H. Sludt 3–32 W. F.M. Whitelaw 3–39

Match Drawn

More Triflers

The guesting Eric Heard, a nephew of Cardinal Heard (the only English Cardinal ever to row in the Boat Race!), was in fact a regular Trifler in the summer holidays and was a Prep School Headmaster in Lancashire. At Lyminster, Eric Heard was known as 'Uncle Eric', earning his title, according to Vi Brown, not by seniority but by his

…imperturbable rosy urbanity. He was our stock uphill fast bowler, unshaken by any mishap. The story ran that Beer was Best for Eric and that a short drink at lunch time might spell disaster – he certainly bowled so many wides in one over that it is said the captain grew anxious lest he should never be able to take him off!

The Stocker named in the score sheet was John Dexter

Stocker, knighted in 1973 and Lord Chief Justice of Appeal from 1986 to 1992. In the Triflers team we see the first appearance of Bob Flood, whose family lived in Lyminster. He was at Lancing College and Reading University in the 1935–39 period. Bob Flood joined the Berkshire Regiment in 1939. He was a Major in the 6th Airborne Division (8th Platoon). In 1958, he joined the 44 Parachute Brigade where he became a Brigadier. In 1965 he was appointed Assistant Commander of the Sandhurst Military Training establishment. He played for the Triflers throughout the 1930s. Bobby Flood's brother John was my parent's best man at their wedding in 1951.

Chapter 15

1938 – 'Peace in our time'

On March 12th, 1938, Austria was annexed by Germany. Two soulmates were reunited, not only by a common culture, history and language, but also by a shared belief in Nazism and its evil intentions. Another part of the Versailles Treaty had been sneered at and clinically broken by Adolf Hitler. The move towards the unthinkable was rapidly happening in front of the noses of the old Allies, France and Britain. The Triflers would soon be pitched into war against their goose-stepping contemporaries in Europe; many would never grow old, never to return to the England of their youth.

Very quickly, Hitler moved to complete the Nazification of Austria, the population of which were willing accessories in a crime against humanity. Hitler passed a law on June 26th giving Austrian Jews two weeks notice to quit their jobs.

An Australian visit

In March, my Australian grandmother's parents, the Metheralls, came to stay at Lyminster. It was the first time that she had seen her parents since leaving Melbourne harbour in January 1931. They stayed for nine months in the atmosphere of a growing European crisis. The four Coopers and two Metheralls set off on their first real holiday for years in the five-seat Morris 12! Cecil Cooper visited his old Finchley childhood holiday haunts of Clovelly, Lynton and Lynmouth before the Metheralls met their long-lost Cornish cousins, the Brents, who were farming near Launceston. The whole trip was a very emotional reunion for Linda Cooper, having not seen her parents for seven years.

Over fifty years later, Polly Cooper returned to the same farm in Cornwall. Her knock at the door was answered by a fully fledged nudist! Polly was not at all thrown by such barefaced cheek! A colony had been established at the residence.

Don Bradman's Australian touring team arrived to do battle for the Ashes in 1938. It was a very significant tour, when the bitterness surrounding the 'Bodyline Tour' of 1932–33 could be finally put to rest. It must be remembered that diplomatic relations between the two countries were nearly broken off as a result of Douglas Jardine's 'Leg Theory'.

1938, Clovelly. Great Grandpa and grandmother Metherall (centre), with Richard and Polly Cooper.

Picnic on the Sussex Downs. From left; Richard Cooper, Cecil Cooper, Polly Cooper and Linda Cooper.

Catch! Richard Cooper at St. Nicholas Prep. School, Littlehampton. The Reverend Flood's house is in the background.

Daphne Byrne

During the war, Land Girl Daphne Byrne was based near Lyminster and used to visit Aunt Vi Brown, thus forming a lifelong friendship. Daphne was not a stereotypical Land Girl. She was the daughter of a Captain RN and later became Secretary to the Bursar of Girton College, Cambridge. An avid writer of articles and stories to the present day, Daphne clearly remembers the day when she met a famous English cricketer:

As a skinny and spotty 12 or 13 year old, my father Captain Byrne RN introduced me to a 'very important' man. We took an instant dislike to each other and I saw him last on a TV film and did not alter my impression. It was D. R. Jardine, the cricketer.

During the 1932–33 tour, Jardine instructed fast bowlers Larwood and Voce to fire short-pitched deliveries on a leg-stump line at the bodies of the Australian batsmen. As many as five fielders waited like vultures in catching positions behind and in front of the wicket. On their return to England, it was Larwood who was ordered by the MCC to apologise to the Australians, not Mr Jardine! He was merely following orders, an ex-miner turned 'professional' cricketer finding himself caught in the intangible world of English cricket enmeshed in the class system. Amateurs were addressed as 'Mr' and the professionals travelled in second-class rail carriages across Australia, separately from their 'betters'. Harold Larwood never lost his dignity by selling his story about these times, he simply emigrated to the country where he had caused such an uproar. Definitely a 'Pommie' who never whinged!

It would be a full 42 years before Australia got their own back on the fast bowling front when Lillee and Thompson terrorised Amiss, Boycott and the rest on the

1974–75 MCC tour. Only Tony Greig stood defiantly in their way, slashing 'Tommo' over the slips and signalling his own boundaries for the benefit of the Sydney 'Hill'.

The 1938 Ashes

Grandpa Cooper wrote regularly to his old solicitor, Herbie Blair, back in Manangatang, Northern Victoria. He concluded one long epistle with a review of the Test match at Nottingham. Grandpa had written at length analysing the European crisis before he moved on to the Test, using many military metaphors to describe the state of play:

That's the end of current history as seen by the man in the country lane, with his limited opportunities for getting at the truth. A better natured war is now in progress at Nottingham. England started with an immense advance from Mons, but met their Marne when McCabe brought up his big guns. Further attempts at English advance have resulted so far (after lunch, 4th day) in trench warfare of the grimmest sort. We don't seem able to take a foot of Australian trench, and are wondering whether the Aussies are going to accumulate sufficient stores for an attack across the open after tea. It will grand cricket if they do. We all thought Paynter's effort hard to beat, but he was coping with bowlers who had their fair share of battering. McCabe on the other hand, had to take on bowlers with their tails up, and Union Jacks fluttering on the breeze. I think it is generally felt that his innings has never been surpassed.

Grandpa Cooper's reference to the Nottingham test match reflected on two brilliant innings, one of 208 by Lancastrian Eddie Paynter, and one of 232 by popular Australian vice captain, Stan McCabe. The test series was a classic which reached an exciting climax in the last two tests. The third test had been completely washed out before the Aussies won a close match by five wickets in the fourth encounter. In the last test at the Oval, England scored more than 900 runs in the first innings, with Len Hutton hitting a then world record 364. England tied the series after winning by an incredible innings and 579 runs.

The first two games of the cricket season at Lyminster saw the Triflers pit their skills against the local rivals Steyning and an invitation side raised by J. A. Macdonald. As conversations increasingly reflected the growing crisis on the continent, the peaceful atmosphere at the cricket ground was a balmy antidote to the strife being unleashed on Europe by Hitler. Perhaps a lot of folk merely wished not to contemplate another Armageddon, happy to ignore the peril of possible war.

May 7th, 1938

The Triflers' CC			**Steyning CC**		
H.G. Crabtree		11	D.A. Ansell		0
J.F. Turner		2	H.E. Adcock	N.O.	53
R.C. Bates		69	P.J. Pafford		1
J. Alderson		6	D.S. Flowers		0
Cap. J.F.B. Barrett RN	N. O.	69	E.W. Mitchell		10
A. Hill		0	R.A. Charman		3
C.C. Cooper		26	F. Allfrey		10
J. Tomset	D.N.B.		C.H. Gillam		9
J. Wool	D.N.B.		R.E. Worsfield		0
G. Weller	D.N.B.		E.J. Cox		0
J.A. Macdonald	D.N.B.		Dr. Dingemans		4
Total	184 for 6 wickets declared		**Total**	90 All Out	

E.W. Mitchell 2–31
R.E. Worsfield 2–37
C.H. Gillam 2–31

J.A. Macdonald 4–33
J. Wool 4–20

The Triflers won by 94 runs

A stand of 86 runs between Capt. John Barrett RN and Cecil Cooper complemented excellent earlier work by PC Bates, whose 69 runs was the highest score of the match. The following game against Godalming saw skipper John

Alderson score a typically quick-fire 74, putting on 101 runs for the third wicket with opener Francis Pagan in double-quick time. The ensuing batting collapse resulted in a defeat of 66 runs against a strong Godalming club XI.

Trifler John Alderson

John Alderson lived in a flat at Lyminster House. He worked at Lloyds, along with CNB. In 1938, John became engaged to my father's cousin, Diana Burgin, daughter of the Rt. Hon. Leslie Burgin and Dorothy Burgin, my great-aunt and sister of my Grandfather Cooper. They married on the outbreak of war the following year, his former Maths master at Westminster School officiating. Vi Brown remembers John Alderson as enthusiastic, impetuous, romantic, untiring and intelligent in everything he did. At Lyminster he carried out an ingenious scheme of hatching out troutlings in a meat safe under a dripping tap in a wash hand basin! He also planted his own white rose on the island in the pond, reflecting his Royalist, Jacobite beliefs.

John Alderson the cricketer was the true expression of John the man. His play was exciting to watch from the moment he went in. He looked for runs from the very start, and if this sometimes led to disaster it lead far more to a fast-scoring innings of well played shots. He not only recognised half-volleys but treated them as such – in fact he hit a fast bowler of repute for a straight in the first over he received so that the surprised opponent said 'Who is this chap?' His freedom, and an unusually consistent coordination of hand and eye gave speed and power to his shots, even before he had reached his full height of 5 7.
Early photographs of John at Westminster School show that his newly acquired top hat was almost taller than him! His square cuts whizzed to the boundary just as his shots at goal whizzed into the soccer net, in much the same way as,

over 60 years later, Sarah Malin, the granddaughter he would never grow old to see, made her television debut on the ITV series *The Knock*. Her red hair and energetic entry onto the set would remind any surviving Trifler today of her grandfather.

John Alderson was also a mainstay of the Lyminster House side along with his fiancés' uncle, Cecil Cooper, making sure village folk felt at home and enjoyed the Lyminster scene a much as The Triflers. He was gazetted into the Seaforth Highlanders on the outbreak of war, seeing action in Madagascar, India and Persia, and then joined the Special Forces Commando Unit, fighting in Italy. As a Troop Commander in No. 3 Commando, landing on Sword beach, he gained the MC, before being badly wounded on D-Day+2. John Alderson was determined to get back to the war in order to see the crossing of the Rhine which he had put his heart on. His especially poignant death just before the end of the war is recorded later in this book.

Keep your eye on the ball!

J. A. Macdonald brought an invitation team to Lyminster on May 28th, 1938. A combination of Triflers and Lyminster House players saw a close game end in victory for Macdonald's side. Two outstanding performances by J. F. Turner (78) and Cecil Cooper (6–24), were not enough to match Macdonald's men, who bowled and batted with consistency throughout the side. The Lyminster House games were often full of gentle humour and moments of eccentricity. When J. A Macdonald and Cecil Cooper played together, field placing was carefully done as they both were an eye short. Harold, the umpire, stood with a crutch in place of one leg. A cricketing scene from village life of the 1930s.

The Scottish Tour started on Monday, June 13th and the following games provided some first class entertainment. The results were:

Monday June 13th
Manderston CC: 116 (L. Gonet 3–13)
Triflers' CC: 113. (J. Alderson 41; J. Blake 23)
Lost by 3 runs

Tuesday June 14th
Loretto CC: 92 all out (H. Rice 5–28)
Triflers' CC: 113–3 dec. (E. Symes-Thompson 37 N. O.)
Won by 11 runs

Wednesday June 15th
Triflers' CC 162 all out (J. Blake 86) (J. M. McGrigor 4–26)
Edinburgh Academy CC: 119 all out (P. C. Blair 54) (H. A. Craxton 3–4)
Won by 86 runs

Thursday June 16th
Triflers CC: 177–8 dec.(P. Blake 50; H. M. Rice 32; J. Alderson 32)
Berwick CC: 91 all out. (H. A. Craxton 4–22; J. A. Macdonald 3–16)
Won by 86 runs

Friday June 17th
Triflers CC: 199–4 dec. (J. Blake 87; P. Blake 48; H.M. Rice 48)
Scottish Wayfarers CC: 97–9 (H.M. Rice 6–39)
Match drawn

Saturday June 17th
Edinburgh Academicals CC: 258–6 dec. (B.R. Tod 119 N. O.; P.J. Oliphant 46)
Triflers' CC: 185 all out (H.M. Rice 54; J. Blake 30) (R. Tod 4–8)
Lost by 73 runs

A tremendously successful tour was enjoyed, the highlight of which was an aggregate of 266 runs by John Blake in six innings at an average of 44.33.

'Operation Scottish trip' 1938!

The complicated travel arrangements made it well worth all the hours of planning and the many phone calls coordinating the squad of players. In 1938 Vi Brown drove the Daimler, and CNB the Ford V8 van, filled with one or two stalwart supporters and the cricket kit and bags. In London, Edmund Symes-Thompson and trainee surgeon Edmund Gonet of the St George's Hospital XI were picked up at Morden Station. Anthony Craxton was collected at St John's Wood. The travel itself formed part of the legend and excitement of the week. A splendid picnic supper at Harpenden, home of Dorothy and Leslie Burgin, was always well received before spending the night at Bedford. John Blake was collected at Nottingham (he had been to the Trent Bridge Test for one day of the Ashes battle against Australia) dead on time at the spot arranged. Darlington was the next stop to collect Jack Rich, where an advance telephone call to the Percy Arms, Otterburn was made in order to book Sunday night accommodation. On Monday, the border to Scotland was crossed, a great thrill for those seeing it for the first time. Captain Barrett RN was moved to say 'One hundred per cent for Staff Work, Vi!'

The journey home took in a great expanse of both countries beauty and heritage. Vi Brown had to follow Freddie 'Thunderbum' Whitelaw (so named after his ample fast bowler's backside) in his equally fast Wolseley: she surpassed herself and beat her land speed record, touching the never-to-be-repeated 70 miles per hour! CNB's van and old Morris driven by Edmund Symes-Thompson, who carefully negotiated the drive through the Moffat Hills made treacherous by sleeping sheep which littered the steep-sided border valleys. Skilful use of the gears by Edmund negated the need to test the brakes of the old Morris! The western route was taken from the Moffat hills, passing Liverpool, the Welsh Borders and Gloucester before taking the old Roman road through Wootton Bassett to Newbury. The last leg of the 386-mile journey passed through Petersfield, dropping off John Blake and his brother in Havant, before the tired remnants of the team found Lyminster House and the loyal Maud Cooper waiting with reviving cups of tea and sandwiches.

Munich

August 15th, 1938, was a momentous date in English history. Prime Minister Neville Chamberlain flew to Munich to meet Hitler seeking certain guarantees regarding Poland. Was Chamberlain resigned to the fact that Hitler would take the Sudeten Germans back into the Reich? Or did he persuade the Czech government to cede the territory, knowing that it was in Britain's interests of buying time to do so? It has been suggested that the Czech army was more than capable of putting up a fight. Hitler was far from finishing the rearming of his own troops and might not have wanted a war in Czechoslovakia. Having said that, Hitler did not like Chamberlain 'drawing his teeth' and being manipulated by him. We have to remember that the policy of appeasement must be understood in the light of the fact that Chamberlain had told Parliament that we were not in an economic position to fight a major war.

Britain, France, Germany and Italy signed the Munich Pact on September 15th, which agreement peacefully ceded the Sudetenland. Chamberlain thought the Munich Pact would satisfy Hitler's lust for territory, but he would be proved sadly wrong. Hitler felt cheated that he'd not been allowed his war in Czechoslovakia. In return for the Sudetenland, Chamberlain guaranteed the protection of Poland. In reality, what on earth could we have done in a practical, military way to defend Poland? The events of September 1939 would bear this out.

He flew back to England sincerely believing that he had brought 'Peace in our time' as he waved the infamous piece of white paper on landing at Croydon Airport. Chamberlain was attacked in Parliament by the Labour MP Herbert Morrison, who said that the Government's retreat from the League of Nations now brought Britain to the edge of war in 1938. The Minister of Transport, Leslie Burgin, replied,

> He [Chamberlain] has talked of the League of Nations and of collective security, and he has given us assurance as to what security could be guaranteed.

Loud cheers reverberated around the Commons. Ironically, founder Trifler Alan Campbell-Johnson had just completed his biography of Anthony Eden in 1938. Eden had resigned as Foreign Secretary in Chamberlain's Cabinet on February 20th, believing that Britain should rearm as soon as possible. Eden later rejoined the Cabinet in the same post when Churchill became Prime Minister in May 1940.

On August 19th, Francis Pagan and Dermot Milman

put on 113 for the first wicket against Worthing, Edmund Symes-Thompson with 36 and Dick Evers's 50 not out resulted in the Triflers declaring at 203–3 wickets off only 35 overs. Worthing struggled in reaching 106–6 in reply. The games against Worthing were synonymous with great cricket battles against J. K. Mathews, a tremendous Sussex club cricketer. Mathews was later a Vice-President of Sussex CC, being a committee member at the 1947 crisis meeting at Hove attended by over 1000 members who met to discuss 'Billy' Griffith's resignation as captain.

The following day Pagan (52) and Milman (48) created Triflers history when, for the second time in two days, they put on 100 for the first wicket partnership against the Sussex Club and Ground XI. The Triflers just hung on to escape with a hard earned draw, being 136–9 at stumps. The Sussex team had scored 226–6 declared, with county batsmen J. Oakes (63) and Collins (77) making the bulk of the runs. Pagan and Milman's great scoring feats were recorded in the *Cricketer* on September 10th, 1938. In an interesting review of the Triflers' season, it stated:

1938 "Watching from the ha-ha" Linda Cooper far right.

In several of the Triflers' fixtures this year the eight ball over was tried; its reception was mixed, but probably the majority of opinions were rather in favour. Much time was saved but a few of the faster bowlers began to feel the added strain, especially in an over containing a no-ball.

The Cricket Week at Lyminster was favoured with excellent weather, only half a day's cricket at Bognor being lost. There were some extraordinary displays of hitting, notably R. P Nelson's 48, composed of six 6's, two 4's and two 2's; in the game against A. L. Hilder's XI 479 runs were scored in just over four hours cricket, 300 coming in boundaries. Against Worthing and against Sussex Club and Ground, on two successive days, F. E. Pagan and D. L. K. Milman added over 100 for the first wicket.

Dermot Milman

Dermot Milman had been educated at Uppingham and Corpus Christi, Oxford. He was a predecessor of Francis Pagan's for a year or two as a schoolmaster at Epsom

College. Milman left for St John's, Leatherhead, when Epsom wouldn't give him a term's leave to play rugby for England in South Africa. He was capped five times as a back-row forward from the Bedford club, playing against Wales (1937–38), Ireland (1938) and Scotland (1938). Milman later served as a diplomat in the British Council overseas from 1946 to 1976 and was knighted for his services to Britain overseas.

German dialogue

In October, Neville Chamberlain gave Leslie Burgin and Sir Samuel Hoare the task of keeping an open dialogue going with the German Ambassador to Britain. In the second half of the month he was taken to secret locations in the country. It must have been a lost cause, but the follow-up to the Prime Minister's Munich trip was an important part of the strategy of appeasement. Prolonging the continuation of dialogue between Germany and Britain was seen as the only real alternative to all out war.

Mid-December saw Linda Cooper's parents return to Australia, their trip to Tilbury delayed by a fierce snowstorm – the first time that they'd ever seen such weather! Grandfather Metherall sent a short note to my father, which ended,

These are still tense times the whole world over, but we have implicit faith in our glorious Empire. Here's hoping that everything will be straightened out to our entire satisfaction.

Love to all at Lyminster,
Grandfather Metherall.

A loyal Australian if ever there was one!

Chapter 16

1939 – 'I have just spoken on the phone to the Prime Minister…'

Adolf Hitler and Mussolini had signed the 'Pact of Steel' on May 22nd, 1939. Hitler would threaten Western Europe if the nightmare scenario happened of an agreement between himself and Joseph Stalin. Germany would not then have to fight a war on two fronts, or not until they were fully ready to attack the sworn enemies of Nazism in the USSR. 'Jaw-jaw' still prevailed over the inconceivable thought of another conflict, only 21 years after the war to end all wars had been fought in Europe.

At Lyminster, the last ever season of cricket was about to begin. Every match from the last Triflers score book has been recorded in this chapter.

May 6th
Lyminster House XI: 110
Storrington: 99 (J. A. Macdonald 6–25; CC Cooper 2–26)
Won by 11 runs

June 3rd
Littlehampton: 241–8 dec (B. Morley-Brown 144; J.A. Macdonald 5–91)
The Triflers: 182–5 (G. Crabtree 56; G.J. Kerr 57 N. O.)
Match Drawn

Scottish Tour
June 12th
The Triflers: 172–7 dec (G. Killick 34 N. O.; W.R. Evers 32)
Manderston CC: 165 all out (W.R. Evers 5–66)
Won by 7 runs

June 13th
The Triflers: 222–6 dec (C. Bell 54 N. O.; D. Milman 46; P. Blake 39; G. Crabtree 36)
Loretto CC: 164–8 (S.J. Hutchinson)
Match Drawn

June 14th
The Triflers: 200–6 dec (G. Crabtree 74;C. Bell 62 N. O.)
Edinburgh Academicals CC: 179–6 (J. A. Eadie 54; J .A. Macdonald 5–42)
Match drawn

June 15th
Berwick CC: 88 all out (C. Bell 4–29; G. Killick 4–17)
The Triflers: 90–3
Won by 7 wickets

June 16th
Scottish Wayfarers CC:185 all out (G. Waterston 41; R. Knight 36; R. Scott 34; P. Blair 27)
The Triflers: 186–4 (J. Alderson 51; G. Killick 49; D. Milman 22)
Won by 6 wickets

June 17th
The Triflers: 263–8 dec (J. F. Turner 148)
Edinburgh Academicals CC: 264–5 (A.J.S. Macpherson 153 N. O.; P.J. Oliphant 53no)
Lost by 5 wickets

The aggregate of 527 runs scored in the last game of the tour against the Edinburgh Academicals was a record in Trifler history. A. J. S. Macpherson's century is also recorded in Sir Michael Woodruff's autobiography *Nothing Venture, Nothing Win*. Macpherson was later a surgeon colleague of Sir Michael's in Edinburgh after the latter's return from the notorious Changi POW camp.

June 24th
Steyning CC: 227–1 dec (N.E. Adcock 112 N. O.; A. Ansell 69; H.V. Chapman 34 N. O.)
Lyminster House XI: 84–4. (J. Alderson 48)
Rain stopped play.
Match Drawn

July 9th
Refreshers: 286–9 dec (Whitehead 105; J.A. Macdonald 4–110)
Lyminster House XI: 223–8 (G. Killick 67; R. Bates 38; J. Alderson 38; W.R. Rees-Davies 4–52)
Match Drawn

July 20th (2 innings match)
Lyminster House XI: 61 all out (E.J. Stanford 8–27; H.A. Stanford 2–12)
Slinfold CC: 111 all out (A.C. Christmas 4–37)
Lyminster House XI: 117–7 dec (Hon. F.R. Rea 20)

Slinfold CC: 39–8
Match drawn

July 23rd
Ashtead CC: 185 all out (J. Cocks 61)
The Triflers: 161 all out
Lost by 24 runs

August 12th
Slinfold CC: 181 all out. (A. Hill 6–26)
The Triflers: 38 all out (W.H. Stanford 7–13; E.J. Stanford 3–11)
Lost by 143 runs

Johnnie Johnson, Slinfold CC

This comprehensive hammering by Slinfold was one of the heaviest ever defeats inflicted on the Lyminster side. A fine knock of 72 by 16-year-old batsman Johnnie Johnson was ended by the slow left-armer Hill. Johnnie Johnson still remembers that innings today. He started off in the Slinfold Club scoring the matches and sitting to next to that 'very pleasant lady, Mrs Brown' throughout the 30s. Johnnie vividly recalls the magnificent cricket teas in front of the large 'Visitor's Pavilion'! In 1938 during one Triflers' game, prolific Slinfold batsman Jack Broadley broke his brand new bat clean in two just below the splice. This did not stop him scoring 86! Johnnie Johnson had made his first appearance against the Triflers as a 15-year-old in 1937, scoring 29 not out. He returned to Lyminster during the war when he was based at Ford, where he was assigned to the job of picking up fragments of the many aircraft shot down over the Sussex countryside. Johnnie recalls Lyminster House adopting an Open House policy to all the Armed Forces. The bare minimum was a warm cup of tea to any member who was passing the house along the A284. Today, aged 76, Johnnie is the stalwart of the Slinfold club, being groundsman and doing 101 other jobs, a scenario repeated by similar bastions of cricket all over the whole country. Will there be a new generation of Johnnie Johnsons in sports clubs over the country?

Lyminster Week (August 18–25, 1939)

The atmosphere at the annual Lyminster Cricket Week was tempered by the impending political crisis. Would the gathering Triflers and spectators ever meet again on the ground at Lyminster? The continuity and stability of village life would shortly be blown apart by the catastrophic outbreak of war, a scene repeated all over the nation.

Rt. Hon. Leslie Burgin

The Right Honorable Leslie Burgin
(First Minister of Supply) Husband of Dorothy Cooper.

Leslie Burgin was the favourite Uncle of Polly and Richard Cooper. Polly Cooper remembers him:

…always shaking us by the hand and leaving a ten shilling note in our hot, warm little paws!

A year's pocket money in the 30s! The Burgins arrived en masse on Friday August 18th, 1939, for the first game of the Lyminster Week. The Triflers were playing the Dragons, a team of Old Boys and guests from St George's School in the Burgins' home town of Harpenden. Leslie Burgin was one of the most talented all-round athletes in Parliament, playing cricket for the Commons and Lords teams, as well as being a good golfer and skier. He often took his family to Lyminster to watch the Triflers' August week.

There had been much discussion of the impending political doom. Breakfast was much quieter than usual on that first morning of the cricket week as the Triflers tucked into their pre-match fare, when Leslie Burgin greeted them with the news:

> I have just been speaking on the phone to Mr Chamberlain [on holiday in Scotland] and he is sure the crisis will soon blow over.

Leslie Burgin had married my great-aunt Dorothy 'Dolly' Cooper in 1912. Like Cecil, Atholl and Basil Cooper, he was educated at Christ's College, Finchley. A keen sportsman, he played for the House of Commons Cricket XI. Burgin had played in the same Finchley football team as Frank Woodruff (brother of Sir Michael's father Harold) and Uncle Cecil Brown. These men met the Cooper sisters through the Methodist Church in Finchley. Burgin then attended London University gaining a 1st Class Hons. in LL.B. During the First World War, he was an Intelligence Officer, being mentioned in despatches, and won the Italian Croce de Guerra. He was a prosperous solicitor with Denton, Hall and Burgin, who had offices in Gray's Inn and Paris.

Leslie Burgin was elected Liberal MP for Luton in 1929, before joining the National Liberals in 1931. Appointed as Parliamentary Secretary to the Board of Trade in 1932, he became Minister of Transport in 1936. He saw fit to spend a night in a lorry travelling on the A5 London to Birmingham road, reaching the conclusion that it was only a minority of private motorists who drove badly, exonerating the castigated lorry drivers from public accusations of recklessness. Travelling back on the Manchester to Euston express on the footplate, Burgin was eager to experience the realities of life aboard public transport. He also travelled the canals and toured the harbours as part of mobilisation plans in the event of a possible war.

There had been political and media demands for a Minister of Supply to be appointed as early as 1936, but Neville Chamberlain had stubbornly refused, stating that British rearmament plans were satisfactory. It was really far too late for Leslie Burgin to make up for so much lost time when he took the post on April 20th, 1939, ironically the date of Adolf Hitler's birthday. It was the first ever such appointment in British history. Chamberlain had stated in 1936 that:

A Minister of Supply would not be calculated to facilitate or increase the rate of completion of the Government programme of rearmourment.

The book *Guilty Men* by 'Cato' (three London journalists – Michael Foot, Frank Owen and Peter Howard) perhaps unfairly includes him on the list of those who had failed in preparing Britain for war, citing the disastrous Dunkirk debacle as evidence of our unprepared military war machine. They wrote:

...and the Government had to be slapped and kicked and cursed and brought to a point where its destruction seemed imminent, before it yielded to the clamour or a Minister of Supply.

Leslie Burgin had been handed a 'poisoned chalice'. The debacle of Dunkirk in the following year would show that years of proper preparation and production of the necessary equipment had been needed. A few months was a matter of too little, too late. It was rather a large can to carry. His greatest mistake during his short term in office was not to include the trade unions in discussions in Whitehall regarding the manufacture and supply of goods in a war situation. All aspects of British industry needed to be singing from the same hymn sheet in 1939.

As the Triflers left the breakfast table to change for the match, none of them really believed Leslie Burgin's optimistic words. They chose to contemplate the situation in quiet reflection. The immediate business was with the Dragons of Harpenden, the home town of the Burgins. Pat Burgin kept wicket for the Dragons and was an occasional Trifler.

August 18th, 1939

The Triflers			The Dragons		
F.E. Pagan		16	J.C.G. Abraham		2
J. Alderson		17	M.P. Nelson		0
A. Christmas		5	D.C.V. Watts		0
J.A. Eadie		5	M.L. Dyson		5
J.S. Brown		1	R.P. Nelson	N.O.	43
S.T. Hutchison		36	R.F.A. Wade		8
Cap. J.F.B. Barrett		26	P.L. Burgin		4
L.W.K. Brown		0	E.W. Pellant		1
A.R.E. Hill		11	R.E. Hunter		0
Hon. F.R. Rea	N.O.	5	J.L. Hatt		0
W.E. Heard		0	K.G. Harvey		4
Total 182 all out			Total 76 all out		

R.P. Nelson 5–49

W.E. Heard 5–16
A.R.E. Hill 4–51

The Triflers won by 106 runs

The Hon. Findlay Rea

The Triflers were captained by The Hon. Findlay Rea

for this final week. He was not among the early Triflers, and when he joined he impressed Vi Brown:

…more by his mordant tongue, which was rarely still, than by his cricketing skill. But we soon found he was and will always be a cricket fanatic, knowing the game, its history and the tactics best employed to exploit or counteract the strength or weakness of both friends and enemies. His captaincy was happy for all, and in the balm of satisfied ambition he mellowed.

Aunt Vi had a lovely turn of phrase on occasions! Rea later found further satisfaction and reward in his post at the *Cricketer* magazine, organising the competitions run by that journal.

Trifles CC Lyminster House 1939. Cecil Cooper, Dick Evers, Eric Heard, Bill Thorburn, Andrew Christmas.(standing)   Francis Pagan, Hon.Findlay Rea, Cecil Brown, John Brown, Jack Rich (seated). Paddy Gawthorne and J.A. Eadie (front row).

The Triflers' match against Havant the following day was also won easily by 92 runs, Francis Pagan's 50 proving the vital innings. A great game versus the Kenya Kongonis followed on August 20th, the Triflers' 222 (J. Eadie 87 not out) proving too high a total for the touring side. Old Dovonians were similarly dispatched on the 21st, with Dick Evers (72) and Findlay Rea (54) being the match winners for the home team. The Bognor XI provided the Triflers' fourth victims of the week on August 22nd, Francis Pagan (59) and Paddy Gawthorne (112) putting on 131 for the first wicket. J. Stallibrass's 117 not out dominated the Bognor innings in their reply of 180, leaving he Triflers winners by 95 runs. Played four, won four! Could they keep up the winning run? Never before had all seven matches been won during a Lyminster Week.

All thoughts of cricket paled into insignificance on the morning of Wednesday August 23rd, 1939. News of Hitler's non-aggression deal with Stalin, the Molotov-Von Ribbentrop Pact was just breaking, blowing a large hole through Leslie Burgin's hopeful words earlier in the week. The Triflers had to make a quick decision. Should they remain at Lyminster and see out the rest of the Cricket Week? Stay they did – they would not have been Englishmen if they hadn't! The thought of remaining unbeaten in all seven games was a welcome diversion from the threat of a second European war in 21 years.

The last home match: the Sussex Martlets CC

On the disastrous day of the German-Russian non-aggression pact, the Triflers gathered for what would be the last game of cricket ever played on the beautiful Lyminster ground. The visitors were the famous Sussex Martlets team. Back in 1932, Francis Pagan had won the first ever Triflers' match single-handedly, and seven years later he repeated the feat, scoring 55 and taking 3–33. His performance sealed victory by 45 runs for the Triflers, their fifth in a row. The penultimate wicket to fall at Lyminster was that of guesting Martlet Cecil Cooper, who was caught by Paddy Gawthorne off the bowling of Jack Rich. It was my grandfather's last ever game of competitive cricket, a game which was made difficult for him as the loss of his eye hindered his vision somewhat. A stalwart of the Christ's College, Finchley XI of 1907–09, Cecil Cooper was there at the swan song of Triflers' cricket. Jack Rich later became Head of Children's Programmes at the BBC before retiring in 1972. He also played for the Duke of Norfolk's XI in the 30s.

The Worthing match – a great game of cricket!

Only two away fixtures remained. The first against Steyning was won by 63 runs. This left the away game against Worthing on August 25th, and a last chance to do battle with the formidable J. K. Mathews. Reading Aunty Vi's *The Silver Cord*, it is quite clear that Mathews had always tried to 'get one over' on what he considered the 'young upstarts'. True to form, 'J.K.' scored 85 runs in a total of 175 for six wickets declared, leaving the Triflers only 90 minutes to get the runs. Vi remembered every ball bowled as the Triflers set about their nigh on impossible task. Francis Pagan, an opening bat of classical style, scored an almost rustic 17. Then John Blake and J. H. Stallibrass (a Trifler elected earlier in the week, after scoring 117 not out for Bognor) played fast and irresistible cricket. John Blake scored 75 and was out with the total on 155 for four. Everyone hurried – 155 for four, 155 for five, 158 for six, 169 for seven, and no more wickets fell till the match was safely won with a few minutes to spare. Played seven, won seven!

The air was charged with cricket excitement, but the

urgency of what came next and the speed of the dispersal was almost as great as the speed of scoring. The players hardly had time for one last look round at the Lyminster House ground. All thoughts of celebration were blunted by the imminent threat of World War Two. Not enough time even for the annual closing of the Triflers' week when the adults would have to play wrong-handed with a tennis ball against Polly and Richard Cooper over the road in the garden at 'Nyarrin'. One thing was for sure though – cricket never died in the Brown and Cooper families, and it thrives amongst the third generation down in the families of CNB and Vi Brown, Cecil and Linda Cooper.

Friday, August 25th, 1939 (12-a-side)

Worthing CC			The Triflers' CC		
H.S. Mathews	run out	7	F.E. Pagan	bowled Benyon	17
J.K. Mathews	c & b Hill	85	P.P. Gawthorne	bowled Smith	14
C. Steel	c Blake b McIntyre	23	J.F. Blake	c 'JK.' b Mathews	75
F. Wheatley	lbw Bell	24	J.H. Stallibrass	bowled Benyon	2
G.R. Leahy	lbw Bell	15	A. Christmas	st Leahy b Mathews	20
C.R. Ingersol	c Flood b Blake	9	W.B. Thorburn	c 'JK.' b Mathews	2
T. Mathews	N. O.	2	C.R.V. Bell	N. O.	14
W.H.M. Broom	D.N.B.		J.P. Wardle	run out	8
H. G. Smith	D.N.B.		A. A. McIntyre	N. O.	3
A.E. Manyon	D.N.B.		G.R. Flood	D.N.B.	
W.F. Benyon	D.N.B.		A.R.E. Hill	D.N.B.	
R.R. Edwards	D.N.B.		Hon. F. R. Rea	D.N.B.	
Total declared	175 for 6 wickets		**Total**	179 for 7 wickets.	

The Triflers won by 7 wickets, the seventh consecutive victory in Lyminster Week

Only three original Triflers survive today in 2001. This story is a testament to all of them, as well as my family, when they were based in Sussex. It is a story which will never be repeated, but it must never be allowed to be forgotten. It represents more than the passing of a cricket club, more the passing of a now lost England in the era before the Second World War. Hitler stopped play in 1939. Many Triflers perished in that conflict. Their ghosts left to walk the Browns' ha-ha wall, which regally separated their Georgian Mansion from the cricket field. This field is now a vineyard, and the crop of 1930s cricketers in our study were a vintage yield, all great patriots. I'm sure they would approve of the new use for the old ground!

On September 3rd, 1939, Cecil Cooper was listening to the wireless in his home in Church Lane as Neville Chamberlain announced the news that war had been declared:

> This morning the British Ambassador in Berlin handed the German Government a final note stating that unless we heard from them by eleven o'clock that they were prepared at once to withdraw their troops from Poland, a state of war would exist between us.
>
> I have to tell you that no such undertaking has been received, and that consequently this country is at war with Germany. You can imagine what a bitter blow it is for me that all my long struggle to win peace has failed.

Grandpa Cooper's first thoughts were of the 1918 Armistice and the false hope that the Great War had failed in being 'The war to end all wars'. Any ex-soldier would have felt the same. There was a deep sense of déjà vu. He walked slowly but surely down Church Lane, full of the realities which would accompany the new conflict, realities which he knew only all too well.

Chaos at Lyminster Church! Sunday, September 3rd, 1939

Although brought up as a Methodist in Finchley, and with umpteen Ministers on all sides of the family, Cecil Cooper had turned away from the Church after his experiences in the 1914–18 war, joining the British Humanist Movement. His deeply held beliefs were basically Christian in essence though. He politely interrupted the Rev. Duval's morning service at Mary Magdelene Church in Lyminster to announce the news that Britain and Germany were at war for the second time in 21 years. The stunned church, although not really surprised, still took time to take in the consequences of the earth-shattering news. Extra prayers were said, but more drama was added to the whole scene when the air-raid sirens went off.

Iris Jones in *Littlehampton at War* includes the recollections of Geoffrey Wells, one of seven brothers living in Lyminster in 1939. Geoffrey remembered the total panic which ensued, with the congregation making its way to the ha-ha at Lyminster House. The Rev. Duval, however, stopped the exodus as he remembered that the banns for a local wedding hadn't been read! Half the congregation was kept behind, while the other half were in full flight, but duty was seen to be done! This comic scene was straight out of a scene from *Dad's Army*, but the humour of the moment would have been lost on the congregation whose actions simply reflected one community's human reaction to an earth-shattering event.

In February 1999, I visited Lyminster for the first time. In my car was the beautiful leather scorebook, an immaculate record of all the matches played by the Triflers and returning to Lyminster for the first time in 53 years. Each name provided a story to tell. Not quite an Elgin marbles scenario, but poignant all the same. In Lyminster Churchyard, the headstones of many of the people in this book lie as permanent reminders of the era. Next to Professor Sisson and his wife lies their gardener, Mr Bishop, buried as close to their old garden as possible. The inscription on his tombstone is simple and poignant:

He made the flowers grow and the birds sing.

I walked up Church Lane, like my grandfather had done prior to announcing the start of the war. The Bucklands, present owners of the western half of Lyminster House had invited me for lunch, and were brilliant and witty hosts. Major-General Ronnie Buckland, now in his seventies, had been i/c UK Land Forces. Judith started the fabulous Arundel Arts Festival in 1985, and had just been appointed as High Sheriff of Sussex. Sitting in Uncle Cecil's old billiards room with its wonderful oak floor, I spent the afternoon writing up my notes. It was in this room where Auntie Vi held her Tea Dances during the war, a venue for WAAFs from Ford and Tangmere, where radar operators from Poling danced with local soldiers.

I later stayed the night next to the old cricket ground at a B&B and strolled quietly along the pathway of the old ha-ha wall, now sadly filled in. A vineyard grew where cricket had been played. In the outside shed hung a distinctly tatty, antiquarian cricket ball, which must have been at least 61 years old. It had been found in the hedge, a legacy from the 1930s, a very poignant and moving piece of evidence somehow. The whole place was unrecognisable from the time of the Browns and Coopers. Yes, this was a story which had to be told.

Chapter 17

1940 – 'The Battle of Britain'

Let us therefore brace ourselves to our duties and so bear ourselves that if the British Empire and its Commonwealth should last for another thousand years, men will still be saying, 'This was their finest hour.'

Winston Churchill

In May 1940, Vi Brown looked out over the outfield at Lyminster House. The picture was very different to that of previous seasons. Long grasses of various hues and varieties grew where carefully mown stripes of light and dark emerald had formed the picture of the perfect cricket ground. Barbed wire surrounded the north-west corner towards the pond where John Alderson had hatched his troutlings a few years before. The Triflers were spread far and wide in the three armed forces. They were now batting on behalf of England and the Empire, not on the cricket ground at Lyminster. The principles involved dominated both game and war. Only the English can really understand this.

In May 1940, the first summer in World War Two saw Britain in the midst of the deepest ever crisis in its history. The extent of this crisis was not known by the general public. The complete collapse of British power was well hidden from the people behind an outward show of defiance. Dunkirk showed that our forces were ill-equipped to fight the German Panzer units. Chamberlain had known this during the period of appeasement from 1936 onwards, and perhaps expediency dominated his policy. It was all very well to blame the so-called 'Guilty Men' made infamous in Michael Foot's book, but Dunkirk blew apart the collective illusion of the nation that we could still control one fifth of the world's land area and also fight a major war on our own doorstep. Remember that Chamberlain had told Parliament in 1930's that our army was in no position to fight a modern war. If the policy of appeasement has been too harshly criticised with the benefit of hindsight, Dunkirk definitely showed that we should and could have rearmed at a much quicker rate from 1934 onwards.

As a result of the BEF's disastrous campaign in France, the Prime Minister, Neville Chamberlain, resigned on May 10th, 1940. Leslie Burgin followed suit and was replaced as Minister of Supply by Herbert Morrison, grandfather of Peter Mandelson. A power struggle developed throughout May between the Foreign Secretary, Lord Halifax, and Winston Churchill. Halifax had been a passionate appeaser throughout the 30s, and the outbreak of war did not stop his attempts to sue for peace. During the Nuremberg Trials after the war, where the leading Nazi War Criminals were brought to justice, it became public that Halifax had been seeking a peace with Germany throughout May of 1940. It has also been suggested that Hitler could have finished off the BEF at Dunkirk, but gave the British Government a chance to discuss peace terms. Hitler's pact with Stalin was only temporary, and the plan of invading the USSR was on hold. The German Chancellor did not want to fight a war on two fronts in

Europe. Halifax argued in Cabinet that a negotiated peace was far better than a catastrophic defeat. On May 25th, Halifax met the Italian Ambassador to discuss whether Mussolini could be a mediator in any peace talks. The next day, the 26th, saw the final battle which resulted in the total defeat of the French army. Halifax became more insistent. How were we to safeguard our country and our Empire. The original fine moral stance of protecting Poland now seemed light years away.

Halifax proposed the possible ceding of Gibraltar and Malta. Churchill was determined to stick to his principles and carry on an all-out struggle. Everything now really depended on the RAF, but it was reported that the Luftwaffe outnumbered our aircraft by four to one! Churchill thought this to be two and a half to one and since the RAF was four times more successful in the skies, we therefore had air superiority!

The crisis grew deeper on May 28th. There were still 200,000 British and Commonwealth troops on the beach at Dunkirk. These included Triflers Sir Richard Doll who had decided not to risk queing on the long jetty to await the larger Naval ships. He ordered his men to shelter in the dunes further down the beach. They boarded a rowing boat which took them to a waiting paddle steamer which transported them back to England. During the retreat Sir Richard had picked up a small kitten. Tucking it inside his uniform, the kitten stayed with him throughout those days at Dunkirk, through the strafing and bombing of the beach by the Luftwaffe. He was very upset at having to hand it over to officialdom on landing on the south coast. Churchill drew on his background of military history and pronounced that nations which went down fighting rose again. If Britain had made peace at the end of May, it would have been on Hitler's terms. Our stance on Poland in 1939 would have been worthless and undesirable. On

June 18th, Churchill, although holding grave worries about the war situation, gave the famous speech which inspired a nation which was itself beginning to hold doubts about the war. Morale was not as good as it was sometimes portrayed.

By the middle of July, Halifax was despatched to the USA as British Ambassador, a country which he disliked. We fought on. The whole war would now depend on the combat over the skies of south-east England. All over the country, evacuation was taking place. The Triflers' cricket pavilion at Lyminster found a new use, turned into a school for the evacuees by Vi Brown. A local dressmaker taught the elder girls and Nancy Grant, a VAD worker, started a folk dance club to supplement more mundane lessons. Mrs Manser, a London supply teacher who had travelled with the children, was refused recognition from Sussex County Education Authority, who stated that all local teachers should be firstly used. Vi Brown fought on her behalf, and she was joined at the 'Pavilion School' by two ex-head teachers, which was a great success. In the spring of 1940, Sussex became a dispersal rather than a reception area, as the fears of invasion grew. In July, John Brown's wife Nesta and children Andrew and Stevie were invited to stay in America with friends of her father. They were booked on the SS Britannic. It was decided to risk the German submarines rather than the bombing in Edinburgh which had started as early as October 1939.

Nancy Grant

Nancy Grant was a dynamic Australian. In the late 30s, she left the village of Lyminster for Austria where she went to rescue Jews from Nazi persecution. As a leaving present, she gave her husband Ronald, a Harley Street Specialist, a grand piano. Ronald responded by running off with his secretary. They had a child. The situation was further complicated when Ronald Grant's mistress died in a car accident. Nancy's reaction was typical of her selfless spirit. She turned up at Ronald's London club and offered to bring up the child and let bygones be bygones. Ronald, studiously reading *The Times*, peered over his newspaper and tersely remarked, 'I never want to see you again!'

He quickly returned to his paper. Nancy, heartbroken on two counts, flung herself into her VAD work, risking life and limb in the process. Gran Cooper often reflected that she had no fear at all at the thought of being killed. There are many legendary stories of her heroic bravery in the war. Vi Brown had offered her a room at Lyminster House and she stayed there for much of the war. Nancy had been a VAD worker in the first war and kept the same Burberry 'mac' which she had worn in France in WW1. She remained a lifelong friend of the Cooper family and visited Lyminster Farm, Crewkerne, when she was well into her 80s. She was also a gifted artist.

My grandparents decided that my father Richard and his sister Polly should be evacuated to stay with their grandparents, the Metheralls, in Australia on the Government Scheme. They spent the summer of 1940 packed and ready to go to any port in the British Isles at 24 hours' notice. The call never came though: the boat on which they were to be transported was diverted to rescue our troops from the disastrous Norwegian Campaign. Polly and Richard were unaware of this, but it soon became clear that they were not going to leave their parents for a journey onto the high seas. They were totally relieved, much preferring to face the dangers of war with their parents. One of Polly and Richard's friends went with his father to rescue British troops from Dunkirk on May 29th. The dangers of war were fully understood and faced with total equanimity, in fact it all seemed like an adventure to the young Coopers. Bike rides in the Sussex countryside were daily trips to see if any enemy aircraft had been shot down. Tension mounted to a peak when on June 14th the German Army triumphantly entered Paris, rubbing as much salt into the wounds of a country which had humiliated them at the Versailles Peace Treaty.

Invasion scare

Lyminster was right bang in the middle of a possible German landing area! The threat of invasion dominated the lives of folk on the south coast and is vividly recalled in detail by the famous authoress, Rosemary Anne Sisson. Then only 16 years old, she remembered a Police Sergeant staying in their house Churchfields, poised by the telephone to ring through any sightings of German invaders. A machine-gun post was set up in the garden, overlooking the flat plain behind Lyminster Church across to the River Arun and the coast beyond. Her glittering career as a writer never distanced herself from her Lyminster roots and today she owns a flat at Rustington, to where she commutes at weekends from her Fulham home. Rosemary Sisson's poetry is renowned, much of it Lyminster-inspired, from the memories and experiences which this book reflects on.

The high spring tides and flat stretch of shore at Littlehampton made the area particularly vulnerable and the invasion scare reached its peak in August 1940, at the start of the Battle of Britain. John and Yeoma Flood, whose parents were busy with ARP duties on the coast, joined Polly and Richard Cooper, aged 13 and 11, in Vi Brown's cellar at Lyminster House, which had been converted into an air raid shelter by CNB, and had an escape hatch leading up to the front drive. Polly used to sneak up into the house at night to avoid her aunt's snoring, more willing to risk the chance of being bombed! She remembers though, that:

> It was fascinating to steal into the other dark room in the cellar where there were dusty ranks of bottles lay resting on their sides. I always managed to sneak back down to the cellar again before I was missed! There was some hilarity one day when we were down in the cellar during an air raid. Miss Cardo backed down the emergency exit showing a great expanse of Celanese Directoire knickers. This apparition tickled both my brother Richard and Uncle Cecil Brown's Prep School sense of humour. Miss Cardo and her thin little sister were both Girl Guide leaders and stalwarts of my Dad's ARP Volunteer force. These stories illustrate the fact that we were never frightened or worried about what lay in store and everything was treated as a joke by the grown ups, not just for our benefit, but for theirs as well I should think.

It slowly became clear though that Germany was concentrating on defeating the RAF and wasn't going to invade until that objective had been achieved. Cecil Cooper moved from his ARP duties to take over as Commanding Officer of the local Home Guard.

Evelyn Emmet, Amberley Castle: Chief WVS Officer of West Sussex

The Pavilion School closed as the evacuees were re-routed to safer parts of England, and quickly became a machine-gun stronghold surrounded by barbed wire. The threat of Lyminster House being taken over by a Company receded and wartime life settled into a daily routine, with the Browns adopting an Open House policy to any Company in the immediate area. The Ford van, once a cricket bag transporter for the Triflers on their Scottish tour, became a mobile canteen for the WVS. The van was donated on the condition that if there was something left of it, the Ford would be returned to the Browns at the end of the war. It was adapted for its new use under the direction of Vi's old sparring partner, Mrs Evelyn Emmet, Chief WVS Officer for West Sussex. She wrote:

Amberley Castle
August 3rd, 1940

Dear Mrs Brown,
        I do think it extraordinary kind of you both to lend us the van for the mobile canteen. I hope when it is on the road you will go round with it once or twice to see how much pleasure and real help it is giving. I am sure from our experience with the other one that it will be filling one of the biggest needs.

    Yours very sincerely,
    Evelyn Emmet

The van was used throughout the war for a multitude of purposes including one emergency trip to Portsmouth carrying bread which was greatly needed at the height of the blitz. The Ford was returned in 1945 with 'a cheque for £50 towards its rehabilitation'. It had been mainly driven by Miss J. J. Payne of Angermering, who like Vi was an Old Girtonian. The vehicle had been kept in immaculate condition.

The German air raid on Poling and Ford, August 18th, 1940

Legend has it that the summer of 1940 was

particularly warm and sunny, but reality states that it was only May and June that were so, nostalgia overriding the fact that the Battle of Britain summer was quite wet. However, Sunday, August 18th, did turn out a fine and sunny day after early morning mist. Two days before, the Luftwaffe had hit RAF Tangmere hard, destroying six Blenheims, seven Hurricanes and one Spitfire. Unfortunately, this was rather small fry when compared to the events of the Sunday which became known as the bloodiest day in the Battle of Britain. All seemed quite normal and peaceful as Bill Blessed, dressed immaculately in white shirt and tie, took charge of the milking. Sixteen-year-old George Carmen, pristine in white smock and chefs hat, milked and then carefully washed and scrubbed the cows paying particular attention to the tails. Cecil Cooper would encourage his apprentice with 'Well done boy!' for a clean and shining cow. Pride in one's work was everything, part of the rich fabric of country life, understood by everyone who worked the land, where it was possible for worker and farm-owner to coexist in harmony.

Gran Cooper had just left the family home Nyarrin to visit the Chief ARP Warden, Miss Cardo. It was just after 2.30 in the afternoon and a faint buzzing noise could just about be heard, like a distant swarm of bees, but only discernible if you listened really hard. The buzzing grew louder until it was clear that West Sussex was being attacked by the most terrifying machines of the Luftwaffe, the JU87s or Stukas as they were better known when at the forefront of Hitler's Blitzkrieg in Poland and France. In reality, the Stuka was probably the most overrated aircraft in the war, excellent for terrorising civilian populations or bombing military targets ahead of German armoured ground attack, but too slow to cope with air combat against the likes of Hurricanes and Spitfires. In fact, the raid on Poling and Ford was the last time that these planes were used in a serious attack on England by Goering. The Stukas mounted their attacks on Poling and RNAS Ford, while their Messeschmidt 109 escort was set upon by Spitfires from Middle Wallop in Hampshire.

The Stuka still made one heck of a racket though! The skies of West Sussex soon reverberated to the sound of dog fights as Spitfires, Hurricanes and Messerschmidts wove their intricate trails of vapour indicating the paths of their ferocious combat above Lyminster. From Littlehampton to Arundel, a widespread hailstorm of spent machine-gun cartridges rained down on the roofs of houses. The effect was a clattering cacophony of terror, a scenario which Spielberg would be stretched to re-enact even if using all the modern day's special effect technology. The effect on the local population was hair-raising, the reaction of the cows at Lyminster tail-raising! They emptied their bowels in volcanic fashion, all over the newly whitewashed walls, milkers and each other alike!

Lyminster was half way between the Ford aerodrome and the Poling Radar Station – a mile from either as the crow flies. Radar and the skyscraping poles remained a mysterious secret though, being built by men who spent the day hundreds of feet in the air as the pylons rose higher and higher. Poling had some anti-aircraft guns, but Ford, then a Royal Naval Air Station used for instruction, was only very lightly defended.

The events of August 18th, 1940 are well documented by Alfred Price in his book *The Hardest Day* and give vivid descriptions of the day's events. Thirty-one Stukas attacked Poling, where WAAF Joan Avis Hearn stayed at her post beyond the warning of the air-raid shelter siren. She continued transmitting messages, even when Trueleigh Radar Station, ten miles to the east, radioed back to say that the set of coordinates for the German aircraft were directly over the top of her at Poling itself! Eighty bombs fell, mainly around the wooden receiver station, putting Poling out of action until the end of August. The receiving station was badly hit, with the top of one of the masts being broken off. The operations room was saved from any major damage, but the station's early warning radar became inoperative. Luckily, mobile radar units which had been placed on the Isle of Wight gave good back-up to Fighter Command. Other mobile units were rushed to Poling and disaster was averted.

At Ford, there was carnage as the 'All clear' followed the first attack only to be met by a second wave of aircraft which completed the 31 Stukas attacking the station. Many personnel were caught in the open and machine-gunned. Some of the officers' quarters were demolished. Twenty-eight people were killed including a matelot's Irish girlfriend, and 75 were wounded. Five Blackburn Shark aircraft were destroyed, along with five Fairey Swordfish, two Fairey Albacore torpedo bombers and one Percival Procter communications aircraft. The war was literally being fought directly over Lyminster House.

Linda Cooper, returning from her visit to Miss Cardo, saw two aircraft in difficulty and was certain they were going to crash in Church Lane. She threw the flowers collected at Miss Cardo's into the hedge. They would have looked rather out of place whilst arriving at one's burning home. Church Lane was safe, but Pilot Officer Ferguson in Spitfire K9969 was hit by a 109 before colliding with an RDF mast at Poling. He then flew through high tension cables before crash-landing at Norway Farm, Rustington. Ferguson was shocked and wounded, but glad to be still alive. Ferguson became ADC to the Duke of Kent, but missed one trip to Scotland due to having treatment for the injuries sustained during the collision. The Duke's entire entourage was killed when the plane carrying them to Scotland crashed. A second escape for the incredibly lucky

Ferguson. A Hurricane crashed at Toddington Cemetery on the Lyminster side of Littlehampton, completing a terrifying day. Two Stukas crashed near Ford.

The raid was over in just five minutes. The Stukas were now fleeing for their lives and as their 109 cover was engaged by Fighter Command, other RAF squadrons attacked them. It has been estimated that of the 31 Stukas, 12 failed to return and six were so badly shot up that they only just managed to reach French soil By the end of the day, the Luftwaffe had attacked other major airfields in south-east England, concentrating on Kenley and Biggin Hill. A hundred German aircraft were shot down and 138 aircraft of the RAF were destroyed. Before the battle, Germany's total number of fighters stood at 1029 and Britain's at 749. Our bombers were outnumbered by 998 to 471, a number which did not include Germany's 261 dive-bombers. The Battle of Britain raged for the next seven weeks and ultimately ended Hitler's invasion plans.

At the end of the raid on August 18th, an emerging occupant of the Lyminster House shelter exclaimed, 'Arundel Castle has gone!' As the masses of billowing smoke clouds from Ford dispersed, it slowly but surely came back into view. A traditional symbol of Sussex, standing proud against German aggression, 900 years of history providing ample metaphoric resistance against any updated twentieth century re-enactment of previous Saxon and Angle invasions!

Today, RNAS Ford (it later became RAF Ford) is an Open Prison, the place occasionally patronised by some of our modern-day footballers, when they crash their Porsches when a cultural night out after lager has proved a comfort blanket. Sometimes maybe an ex-MP or two find their way to Ford Prison. Perhaps this is the price of progress and freedom fought for by the likes of those who suffered in 1940 during the raid.

The very last Triflers' match: August, 1940

Francis Pagan had gathered together a Triflers' XI for a final game at Ashtead Cricket Club. The game was won for the home team by a famous name in World War Two MI5 history. Sir J. C. Masterman, later Provost of Worcester College, Oxford, had been invited to play by Colin McIver, the Ashtead captain. They had played a lot of cricket together over the years, particularly for the Harlequins XI in the 1920s when they would play two-day matches against the Royal Engineers at Chatham, the Royal Artillery at Woolwich, Aldershot Command at Aldershot, and the Royal Marines, usually at Deal. In one such tour game the opening batsman did not turn up, so Colin McIver was promoted from No.11 in his place. He made 100! This started a Harlequin tradition that whoever went in last in an innings on the annual tour must go in first on the next match! Masterman had been Alan Campbell-Johnson's History lecturer at Christ Church, Oxford. Alan's last four deliveries were hit for 6, 4, 4, 6 by his ex-tutor, who added to the drama by reaching his century off the final ball bowled! Francis Pagan had wanted to provide a cricketing 'carrot' for the Ashtead team to bite at – Masterman nibbled and then devoured the offering and took the Triflers' attack apart. He unwittingly put to bed for eternity the Triflers' Cricket Club, only to remain vicariously as nostalgic memories for future descendants of the Cooper family in years to come.

Sir John Masterman

Masterman, in his wartime job with MI5, had dealings with Bletchley Park, an establishment which has remained a metaphorical 'enigma' for decades. Only now is the truth emerging. It has been estimated that nearly 1,000,000 lives were saved as a result of the brilliant boffins who worked endlessly at breaking the secret code of the Nazis. Years had passed without anybody talking about those times, a testimonial to the values which kept Britain a united nation against the threat of invasion.

In Whitehall, Sir John Masterman's work for MI5 exemplified the pure talent and unadulterated genius of those who baffled the Nazis. Our counter-espionage tactics and the deception of double agents provided proverbial googlies for the Germans, who never were able to unravel the deception, which ultimately led to Germany thinking that Normandy was only a decoy for an invasion in the Pas de Calais. It was Masterman who ran the famous spy 'Garbo'. Maybe our penchant for cricket was an influencing factor in deceiving the Germans! No German agent ever worked successfully in Britain, and many were used as double agents: it was this project which Mastermind was in charge of, although he modestly regarded himself as a 'back-room boy'! He was amazed by the ability of British wireless operators, who could mimic an individual German operator after a year's practice. He also planned 'the man who never was' deception and countless other schemes which hoodwinked the Nazis. It is interesting to note that MI5 never worked so efficiently as during the war, when many intellectuals joined the organisation. Even though they were technically 'amateurs', they added academic rigour to all the business at hand. From the 1950s onwards, our secret service organisations have certainly had their problems, all well documented.

John Masterman won a 1st Class Honours degree in History at Oxford University in 1913. He was interned in Germany during World War One, after being caught unawares whilst studying in the country in 1914.

Masterman was a gifted sportsman, playing tennis, squash and hockey for England. He also went on the 1937 MCC tour to Canada and was elected President of Oxfordshire County Cricket Club from 1956 to 1965. After receiving the OBE in 1944, he was knighted for his services to the Intelligence Corps in 1959. His entry in *Who's Who* refers to his role in the war only as 'Specially employed'.

August, 1940

The Triflers' CC			Ashtead CC		
E.R. Smith		13	J. Reichwald		23
I. Darbyshire		56	C.D. McIver		6
F.E. Pagan		26	C. Weller		28
J.F. Turner		13	K.L.T. James		7
A. C-Johnson		0	J.C. Masterman	N.O.	100
J.E. Facer		0	E. Goldsmith		5
B.A. Smith		28	C.P. Buck		1
Hon. F.R. Rea		15	J. Collier		5
W.E. Gerrish		15	A. Hills		6
C.L.M. McClintock	D.N.B.		S. Harris	N.O.	2
J.E. Rich	D.N.B.		L.D. White	D.N.B	
Total declared	192 for 8 wickets		**Total**	193 for 8 wickets	

Ashtead CC won by two wickets. This was the last ever game played by the Triflers.

August 22nd, 1940: a new crisis.

Churchill's War Cabinet met to discuss an alarming report regarding our gold and exchange resources. It forecast Britain's imminent financial collapse and inability to continue fighting the war. Again, it emphasised that the crisis wasn't made by our defeat in France, but by a gradual decline over two decades. We had too many world wide commitments. We had a lack of peaceful allies, a weak industrial base and too few resources. All this made Britain's survival in 1940 under Winston Churchill all the more remarkable.

German parachutist at Lyminster House, November 15th, 1940

At Lyminster, the autumnal scene was supplemented on November 15th by something rather more sinister than falling copper beech or oak leaves – a German aircraft was in difficulty and a parachutist baled out over Lyminster. The throng of farmyard workers watched in awe as the billowing white canopy gently edged its way earthwards to Lyminster House! At first, Rosemary Anne Sisson thought the German was going to land in the Churchfields garden, but he hitch-kicked his legs rather like an animated Jesse Owens prior to landing in the Berlin long jump pit of 1936. One wonders if the pilot concerned was present at those games – he must have stayed longer than the racially outraged Fuhrer, who pathetically stormed out of the stadium. The downwardly mobile German kicked off one of his flying boots in the process, and tugged his parachute strings just enough to avoid a greenhouse or apple-tree-branch landing! These emergency manoeuvres took him to a softer touchdown with English soil, the precise location being between the lawn and ha-ha at Lyminster House. Grandpa Cooper quickly grabbed a pitchfork and confronted the pilot, who was only too pleased to have escaped death. He was promptly arrested and taken to the house where Vi Brown ordered a cup of tea for the unfortunate soul. This touch of humanity in a barbarous war, caused a division of opinion in the village of Lyminster, but it didn't worry Vi Brown. She had become Billeting Officer for evacuees from London.

The landing of the parachutist prompted the Spitfire pilot who shot him down to jump into his two-seater sports car and make it hotfoot to Lyminster from Tangmere. His arrival, dressed in goggles and flying scarf, certainly enhanced Rosemary Sisson's whole day!

The German pilot was possibly Uffz. Meise flying 4/JGT Bf109 5947: he had baled out over the Sussex coast, and the actual 109 crashed at Felpham. The incident is recorded in John Foreman's *The Battle of Britain: The Forgotten Months, November and December 1940.* If my research is correct, then the English Spitfire pilot was the prolific Sergeant J. N. Glindinning.

236 Field Coy Royal Engineers and the first Lyminster House Tea Dances

The arrival in the Lyminster area of the 236 Field Coy Royal Engineers under the command of Captain B. J. Thompson, was warmly greeted by Vi and CNB. The Company had been part of the Highland Division trapped in France, but they'd managed to escape back to England through Cherbourg. The Browns turned their billiards room into a canteen for the troops and a centre of social activity. This marked the beginning of the Lyminster House Tea Dances, which became very popular with the Army, female signallers from Poling Radar Station, WAAFs from RAF Ford, as well as local girls from the village of Lyminster including Lane the carpenter's three daughters. Sergeant Murray of the 236th brought his bagpipes on many occasions, but more often than not Vi Brown had to tune the crystal radio set into Glenn Miller's dance favourites!

Wartime romances

Many wartime romances blossomed as a result of liaisons which started as dances on the polished billiard room floor. This included the saddest when a quiet, pretty young London girl by the name of Maise married an RAF officer after a broken engagement to a Scottish soldier. He was arrested for bigamy and went to prison, rejected by his existing family. Amazingly, it was Maise who stood by him, visiting him in prison and receiving a loan from Vi Brown to help him in his plight. Sadly, Maise caught scarlet fever and died very quickly. A tragic aside to troubled times.

Usually though the dances were remembered for all the right reasons. They had originally started on Thursdays, because Vi had been told that the soldiers were short of money a day before they were paid and would not be going elsewhere for entertainment. Vi did not really like the associated cynicism associated with this view, but she was happy that the dances became a great success. Percy Mauchan, a Scotsman who frequently sang in a broad brogue, was always a big hit. Corporal Walker was remembered as the most cheerful undertaker that Vi had ever met.

Mrs Fergusson, a 76-year-old neighbour, hired a radiogram to enhance the range of music at the dances. It was such a success that CNB bought it outright, where it remained in the Brown household for years to come, seeing service at Wayford, near Crewkerne, and Bradford Road, Sherborne. Saturday dances were started and one particularly memorable one occurred when Auntie Maud made a cider-cup. Wickedly, she laced it with brandy, causing a visiting Canadian Black Watch soldier to comment:

This is like real Canadian apple-jack – powerful stuff!

Lt. Slater's letter paints a clear picture of that evening, particularly if one understands the understatement of the image being conveyed!

Aldershot
December 18th, 1940

Dear Mrs Brown,

…The party was indeed a tremendous success and beautifully run. You should be a General – because to be perfectly frank, I think you could run certain aspects of a soldier's life much better than an Army office, who hasn't the same knack. Several of the men volunteered the information that it was the best weekend they'd had in England…

Yours sincerely,
Lt. Slater.
Well done Auntie Maud!

The Tea Dances had became the centre of life in these newly formed communities thrown together by the necessity of war. The following year would see the first of many Triflers killed in the war.

From left; John Flood, Reverend Flood, Richard Cooper, Jeff Metherall, Polly Cooper, Mrs Flood, Major Cecil Cooper, Linda Cooper, Yeoma Flood.

Pilot Officer Jeff Metherall (brother of Linda Cooper), Australian R.A.F.visits Lyminster House, 1941.

Chapter 18

1941 – 'Linda…unfinished business!'

Cecil Cooper had fought through the majority of battles in the First World War: in fact he was recommended for the MC for a wire-cutting exercise at the Somme, but both his senior officers were killed before their reports were sent. Cecil's time in Australia had not only seen him battle with drought, but also with the handicap of losing an eye. It was not a logical step, and rather a shock to the family, when he volunteered his services to the army for a second time in 27 years claiming '40/40 monocle vision' as he sought to convince the authorities that they should let him join! Cecil had turned to his wife Linda and merely said,

'Unfinished business!

He entered the Royal Artillery at the rank of Captain. His virtually blind mother, by that time evacuated from Finchley to Limpley Stoke, near Bath, wrote him one of her last letters before her death the following year. She said her mind was quickly thrown back 27 years to early August 1914, when a young, proud and patriotic Cecil announced his embarkation for France. His own late father, Charles, simply started polishing Cecil's new boots, too moved to do anything else.

Linda Cooper was left to run Lyminster Farm and the Guernsey herd on her own, coordinating the work force and acting as an intermediary between them and the Browns, a task which at times needed the skills of a diplomat. Linda always showed tremendous tenacity in a crisis. This was put to the test when her home help, the heavily pregnant Queenie Nurcombe, had to be rushed to Littlehampton Hospital during the blackout. Driving the Ford with hooded headlights in order to comply with ARP regulations, she risked life and limb in the darkness. Picking up a policeman on the way, Linda just made it to the hospital – only just though, because Queenie had the first of her twins on the entrance steps!

Linda's daughter Polly was boarding at Rosedean School in Lampeter, Wales. My father Richard Cooper was due to attend Kingswood School, Bath, which had been evacuated to Uppingham School in Rutlandshire. Kingswood had been taken over by the Admiralty. Linda's own family were thousands of miles away in Australia, the distance only broken by the expected arrival of her brother Jeff Metherall, a Hurricane pilot in the Australian Airforce.

Harvest time was always a special time of year in rural Sussex of the 1940s. Manual labour meant the use of carts pulled by donkeys and horses, a Constable scene if ever there was one. In 1941, Linda Cooper oversaw the bringing in of the hay harvest. Linda was now living in Lyminster House with her children, Polly and Richard, who slept in the Blue room and dressing room. Linda had the old Triflers' 'Dormitory' as bedroom-cum-office. The three of them were joined by all the farm workers, including the ageing Mills who still stacked a mean hayrick at the age of 72! They were joined in that year by 'Tex', a native of that famous state, who'd joined the Canadian Army by claiming Saskatchewan as his birthplace. It must have been a pretty minute harvest when compared to Prairie standards! Even Vi Brown herself joined in and any guests who could be spared. Their transport was a two-wheeled farm-cart drawn by Yevoshenko, an aged horse, supplemented by Jamaica the donkey, who pulled an even more aged cart, with Harold Endersby in tow. The whole experience left a lasting impression on Tex, who later wrote the following words to Vi Brown:

My dear Mrs Brown,
I am back in the same rut at camp and have at last resigned myself to giving up the ease and comfort to which I so quickly accustomed myself while at your home. I wish to thank you for your hospitality, I feel so much better for the visit and what's more important I believe I've learnt something of the art of living pleasantly. (And this in our rationed, restricted wartime home.) You are the most charming hostess I've ever known. Please give my regards to all the family. I've enjoyed their company more than I can say...

Tex

Sadly, news came through to Lyminster that Trifler Eric Bompas, had been killed in action against the Japanese outside Hong Kong. He was posthumously mentioned in despatches in April 1946. Lieutenant Bompas is buried at the Stanley Military Cemetery, just beyond the small fishing village of Stanley in the southern part of Hong Kong island on the Tai Tam peninsula, which has Stanley Bay in the west and Tai Tam Bay on the north.

Chapter 19

1942 – The fall of Singapore and the Dieppe raid

The Americans had entered the war on December 7th, 1941 after the Japanese attacked Pearl Harbour. Three days later on the 10th, the British battleships *Repulse* and *Prince of Wales* were sunk. The Japanese began their advance on Singapore, whose defences were mainly comprised of guns facing out to sea. It was unthinkable that the Japanese army would threaten the British stronghold by the land route. Vi Brown and Cecil Cooper's youngest nephew, Michael Woodruff, was working as a surgeon in the Australian Army Corps in the area. His first battle casualties started to arrive on January 14th, 1942. The unit moved to Singapore Island at the end of the month, where he worked at the Civil General Hospital, operations being performed under the constant barrage of shells. On the 27th January, Michael Woodruff was assisting Lt. Col. Coates with a head operation when a shell hit the roof of the theatre. Sir Michael recounts in his autobiography, *Nothing Venture, Nothing Win* that:

> Mercifully, the shell exploded on impact, neatly removing the roof but not causing serious injury to anyone in the theatre. A day or two after this unnerving experience I was again

assisting Coates when an urgent order was delivered to him in the theatre, ordering him to report immediately to the docks.

Coates was one of a small number of Australian officers who were ordered to return home, taking with them important information about the conflict. Michael Woodruff was left with the instructions to,

Find the maximillary artery and tie it at its origin or, if necessary, tie the external carotid!

The hospital was now totally surrounded by billowing smoke. It was only a matter of time before the inevitable took place. In Singapore itself, the two Indian Divisions and one Australian Division were hopelessly exposed. Winston Churchill later admitted that:

…the possibility of Singapore having no landward defences no more entered my mind than that of a battleship being launched without a bottom.

On February 15th, General Percival surrendered. At Singapore General Hospital, Japanese troops with fixed bayonets tore through the hospital killing 270 patients, including an anaesthetised patient in the operating theatre. The surgeon, Captain Thomas Smiley, RAMC, was bayoneted protecting a patient, but he survived and was awarded the MC. The Japanese Commander, Yamashita, was known as the 'Rommel of the Jungle' and constantly outflanked and out manoeuvred the British troops. After the war he was hanged for the hideous crimes against humanity which he horrendously carried out on a regular basis. One of theses crimes is recorded by Woodruff:

For me the saddest part of the sad story of battle for Singapore was the loss of so many of our nurses. The day before the surrender the *SS Vyner Brook*, carrying sixty-five Australian nurses, was bombed and sunk near Banka Island. Many, including Matron Pasche (10 AGH), Matron Drummond (13 AGH), and Matron Kinsella (2/4 CCS), were drowned. Fifteen managed to get ashore, but were marched to the edge of the water and machine gunned in cold blood. Of the fifteen, there was only one survivor, Sister Bulwinkle (10 AGH), who feigned death and subsequently managed to escape.'

Sister Bulwinkle's obituary was recorded in the Daily Telegraph in the year 2000. Yamashita visited the hospital at Singapore and did allow Michael Woodruff and other medical staff to move the most seriously wounded to Changi. Woodruff became one of 50,000 British and Australian troops interned at the Changi POW camp. He was able to save hundreds of lives at Changi by processing wild passion fruit, Serangoon grass and other grasses into a vitamin and mineral drink. The resulting mixture was foul in taste, but it did the trick, though many men refused to take it.

Nearer to home, Linda Cooper's brother, Jeff Metherall, a Hurricane pilot was on leave from the Empire Air-Training Service. He visited his sister Linda at Lyminster in April. Cecil Cooper was home on leave from the army and all seemed well. In May, Linda received news that her brother had been shot down at Acroma in Libya. The following extracts are taken from a letter to Linda Cooper from Raymond Shaw, a pilot colleague of Jeff's:

Jeff and I have been true friends ever since we sailed from Australia to Canada, and never have I heard anything but praise said against him, particularly from his fellow pilots. He was the finest man I have ever known, totally unselfish, always smiling irrespective of the conditions and weather...

The only consolation I can offer you is that he died in action, in an endeavour to protect another pilot who was being severely attacked by superior numbers and Jeff crashed in our lines and was buried with full military honours by our Army...

Jeff and I flew many times on operations together and he was always admired for his cool head and keenness, particularly when he had bailed out at a very low altitude, with his engines on fire. In many dog fights we have been in Jeff was always the man who, instead of trying to get personal victories himself, protected his fellow comrades and always at great personal risk to himself....

With her children away at boarding school and husband in the army, she had been left to run the pedigree herd and farm, a job she did with great skill and determination. With the news of her brother's death, Linda became very ill with a large stomach ulcer. Months of rest along with a milk and rice pudding diet, ensured her recovery.

At Lyminster, visiting Companies came and went with regularity. These included the Canadian Black Watch; the Cameron Highlanders of Ottawa, with their badge of a polar bear, the Shropshire Light Infantry and Vi Brown's fondest, the Royal Welch Fusiliers under the Command of Captain Elkington. He wrote an appreciative letter to Vi Brown from which the following extract is taken:

Dear Mrs Brown,

...I wish to thank you on behalf of the N. C. O. 's and men of the Company, for the great kindness you have shown them during their stay here...

Your efforts on our behalf are greatly appreciated, the tea dances (some now out on the lawn) have been enjoyed to the full, and the hospitality in allowing the men to use your billiard room was wonderful...We will always remember Lyminster and the pleasant associations we have with it.

V. D. H. Elkington,
Captain,
o. c. 'B' Coy,
8th Bn Royal Welch Fusiliers

What Vi Brown chose to ignore was that Captain Elkington passed a subtle 1940s judgement on the nature of Cecil Brown's wealth. When admiring the huge coat of arms adorning the wall over the main fireplace in the living room he remarked, 'Is that the family coat of arms?'

On hearing that the Browns had acquired it with the house, he remarked with more than a tinge of sarcasm, 'I thought as much!' – a rather snobbish allusion to the fact that the Browns were seen as 'new money'. The RWFs kept the Cricket Pavilion in immaculate order, as three machine-guns were mounted alongside immaculately stacked piles of ammunition. Every item that was lent to the RWFs was returned in perfect working order, including a wireless set which Vi sent to the Officer's mess.

The Shropshire Light Infantry were remembered for their quick step marching and the care of their mascot – a live bear! One member of the Company was a magnificent pianist/singer. His pursuit of music and song continued after the war in London and New York. Vi Brown leaves no record of his name though.

An old friend of Lyminster and elder Trifler, Captain J. F. Barrett, RN, was appointed to the command of an ex-liner. Vi Brown presented him with a collection of old Triflers' stumps and balls in the event of an opportunity to play cricket while ashore on lawful occasions. His command was shortly torpedoed in the Atlantic and sank though nearly making port. The cricket gear and ship's library sank with her – but Barrett lost only two ratings, killed in the original explosion. Captain Barrett had insisted while supervising the conversion of his ship that the sleeping quarters of all his crew should be above the water line.

The growing strength of the RAF was evident in 1942. Participants at the Lyminster tea dances would watch in admiration as squadrons of Sterlings flew in at dusk, almost skimming the trees. Ford became a very important base for the new night-fighter Mosquitoes. At one dance, a Polish squadron of Typhoons, flying in line abreast from Tangmere, eight miles away, nearly sucked the slates off the roof at Lyminster House. Lame ducks from bombing raids were followed studiously as they limped home into Ford aerodrome.

In the summer of 1942 a battalion from the 2nd Division of the Royal Regiment of Canada were billeted in the Lyminster area. Vi immediately contacted Captain Thompson at Company Headquarters to offer a formal hand of friendship in the form of a general invitation to the Lyminster House dances. Thompson handed on Vi's message to Sergeant-Major Holohan. The battalion were a tough bunch, and at their first dance late arrivals who'd been imbibing in the Six Bells in Lyminster joined Pat, Ted and Blackie. A difficult atmosphere prevailed for the rest of the session in the billiard room. Sergeant-Major Holohan met Vi in a debriefing session and promised to 'sort out the boys'. He did not want his troops to damage the house, but perhaps he felt that it was a case of 'what do you expect?' in the circumstances.

Holohan had been born in England of Irish parents, one of an army family of 13, and midway through his teens had become the man of the family, with his father and elder brother away at the last war. Vi and the S-M met on Wednesday, August 19th, he told her that he was a drinker and that the Lyminster dances did not appeal to him:

I won't pretend that it would. I can't flatter women. (although most of them seem to live on it) – if a girl has her hair frizzled up and says, 'Do you like it?' I say, 'No, I think it's horrible'.

A long discussion ensued regarding who should be invited to the Lyminster dances from the battalion. Holohan offered to hand-pick the soldiers he knew he could trust. Vi was adamant though that the atmosphere of the get-togethers would naturally draw those who would respect the occasion. Ever the idealist, Vi enjoyed the frank exchanges with Sergeant-Major Holohan. What happened next added a tragic poignancy to their meeting.

On Friday, August 28th, Scottie knocked on the door of Lyminster House and asked:

Is Ma Brown in? I hear she wants to meet the boys back from Dieppe – I'm one of 13 out of 1,000.

The actual figure may not have been exact, but the Royal Regiment of Canada was decimated like all the other regiments. Canadians who had just a few days previously been quickstepping over the oaken billiard room floor now lay as corpses piled up on the shingle banks of Dieppe beach. Out of 4,963 Canadian troops, 3363 were killed or wounded, captured or missing. The full report on the raid was not released for 30 years. It has been asserted that valuable lessons were learnt concerning landing troops on beaches, especially with a full invasion of Europe in the pipeline at a later date. This theory rather camouflages the fact that it should not have taken a total disaster to learn these lessons. Many historians have stated that it was only a side-show to maintain credibility with the USSR, who were demanding a second front to be opened in the west.

Captain Thompson and Sergeant-Major Holohan went together with the same land mine that the Captain had trodden on. Pat and Ted joined Scottie and Vi at Lyminster House, but there was no Blackie. Ted had been stranded in a landing craft which was being strafed by German machine-gun fire, and Blackie was shot through the head at his side. Company Sergeant-Major James Holohan is buried in the Dieppe Canadian War Cemetery, Hautot-Sur-Mer, Seine-Maritime. There are over 900 war casualties commemorated on this site. His wife and family lived in Toronto.

The Canadians talked and talked to Vi that night, and she listened, visibly shaken and shocked to hear of the carnage which had occurred just a few miles over the Channel from Littlehampton. Ted reported to Vi that:

> We just kept the Navy's orders of a crossfire going and when we had to be got off shore to avoid complete annihilation, we just pulled into the boat those wounded that we could, but it's awful to see your own boys going down. We managed to land no tanks in that first assault and so the machine-gun fire had, for perhaps 20 minutes, free play. Two Churchills were shot in two before they beached.

Many years later Vi got a letter from Sandy, another member of the Royal Regiment who'd been captured at Dieppe:

...I am sorry not have written for so many years, but am only just getting back the use of my hands after working in the salt mines.

Over the next few weeks, the Tea Dances mirrored the Dieppe Campaign. My grandmother was visibly shattered as she viewed the near empty room, so different from the busy scene which had earlier prevailed.

The replacements for the Regiment came from many sources, including literal cast-offs from other units, a situation which caused some unrest. In the autumn though, the 38th Light Anti-Aircraft Battery RCA from central Canada soon made friends with their new neighbours the Browns. Vi received a letter from Doris Lancaster, the wife of one of the troops in the Battery:

...my dear hubby is over there in England...and recently he told me that you were so very kind to the boys in his outfit and that your home was open for them to drop in and have a game of pool (snooker!)...The boys do appreciate your kindness very much and needless to say their wives back home here are very grateful to you also.

...It is 25 below zero tonight, Jack was telling me the grass is still quite green where they are stationed...Perhaps you will write me a few lines. I would be so happy to hear from you...

At weekends Cadet Ratings from HMS King Alfred had for many months formed an especially close relationship with the Browns. They helped in the gardens, joined in Vi's play-reading circles and conversed for hours on a multitude of topics. The young ratings were mainly from New Zealand, South Africa and Australia. At the end of 1942, Vi received a letter from Mr Jordan, the High Commissioner for New Zealand:

On my recent visit to HMS King Alfred I learned with great

pleasure of the kindness which you showed to our New Zealand Naval Cadets who are undergoing instruction in the Establishment.

I much appreciate your hospitality and ask you to accept the grateful thanks of the Government and people of New Zealand.

As well as the Armed Forces, Vi Brown welcomed many others to enjoy the warm hospitality of Lyminster House. Daphne Byrne, remember, was a Land Girl who clearly remembers the happy days at spent at the Browns:

Sometimes of a summer's evening, we (Shelagh Morrisey) cycle over to Mr and Mrs Brown's beautiful house at Lyminster – young farmers and Land Girls mainly – and dance the Circassian Circle or sit out among the roses, reading or drying our hair or just talking. On one occasion, six tennis balls appeared in the sky – parachutes – and then a column of smoke and the old Walrus Seaplane rises out from Ford to locate the crash. (The current joke is that Tangmere shoots down the planes which Ford misses!) One of the farmer's lads brings down a duck in his tin helmet. This calls for drinks all round the pub.

Mrs Brown is full of energy, getting the young motivated, regardless of our need for a quiet life off duty! She and Mr Brown, a quiet, charming man, are the most generous to us all with great hospitality. She was one of the first Girton girls at Cambridge and very keen on the Fabian Society, which is beyond our ken. I think Mr Brown is a Lloyd's Underwriter but am not sure. They could not be more unalike.'

Daphne kept in touch with Vi up to Vi's death in 1970. I discovered Daphne's reminiscences in the West Sussex Records Office in 1999. I tracked her down and we have picked up from there – the clarity of her memory in bringing alive all these events is inspiring. People never forget a kindness, a rare commodity these days, both in terms of the kindness itself and the appreciation shown.

Chapter 20

1943 – 'The beginning of the end'

Sir Winston Churchill's famous words echoed over keenly tuned radio sets throughout Britain. In North Africa, the Eighth Army had captured Tripoli on January 23rd. Eight days later, the surrender of German Field Marshal Paulus at Stalingrad was followed by the Soviets taking Kursk on February 8th. By April, the German Army in North Africa had also met the same fate. The invasion of Sicily and Italy by the Allies in the summer resulted in the Italians unconditionally surrendering in September and then on October 13th declaring war on their ex-Axis partner. A new air of confidence swept the nation, supplemented by the arrival of American troops on British soil.

The American Army

Vi Brown had made many lifelong American friends on her holiday to Virginia and the Carolinas in 1936. These friends were definitely more cerebrally inclined than one GI she encountered at Lyminster. Some lovely conversational exchanges were recorded by her, which reflect more than a simple clash of different cultures, and rather a difference represented by just about the width of the Atlantic!

GI Now we've been over here, perhaps you'll learn to make ice-creams! Of course though, you play football with an round ball, in America we use an egg-shaped one!
Vi I think you will find, if you look hard enough, that we've been playing Rugger for over 300 years!
GI Gee! Yo little ole house would sure make a mighty fine road house. I can just imagine a gambling saloon upstairs and an ice-cream parlour down below!
Vi (No comment, but cheeks flushed bright red.)
GI You have to admit though that we have got the finest system of education in the whole wide world!
Vi Well, why don't you make *use* of it then!
GI Most of our cases in the camp hospital are concerned with treating feet problems.
Vi Is this due to ill-fitting boots?
GI No! We Americans are just not used to walking!
Vi You *did* say that you had the finest education system in world?!

The Browns did actually receive many American guests sent by the English-Speaking Union. To be fair, Vi Brown had found the young GI rather likeable, if extremely crude in the context of 1940s Middle England. The GI had a penchant for wearing yellow gloves and admitted to being susceptible to respectable blondes! Irresponsible blondes more likely.

The ESU guests to Lyminster in the war were many and plentiful. In Vi's opinion, the finest included Margaret from Kentucky, a warrant officer in the Army; a West Point officer from Vermont whose compatriots were missing in the Philippines; a courteous sergeant from Georgia interested in physical training to whom Vi gave her fencing foils, which she hoped would provide a more suitable pastime than the slot machines at the camp; an energetic schoolmaster from Kansas who cycled the Sussex countryside, appreciating its beauty as any boy from his home state would; Tony, an American of Italian parentage, who worked in the office of the Naval Attaché. He was a refined man of immaculate manners, whose sister wrote to Vi expressing the great pride which America had in England. Vi later wondered if this was felt as much in the post-war period. Then there was John with a French surname from near the Canadian border, a jolly light-hearted soul. Jim from Tennessee completed the list. He worked in the American Red Cross, helping GIs who were the victims of the seamy side of London life, being prone to 'sharks' and 'greedy peddlers' of illicit drink. Jim had worked on the Tennessee Valley Project, part of Roosevelt's New Deal for America. The strain of his work in dealing with the lonely, vulnerable soldiers, often in various states of despair, paints a very different picture of London life from that of cheering crowds and 'V for Victory' signs.

Glasgow, 1943. Major Cecil Cooper back left.

'Bad hats and deserters'

The American Army was also a topic of Grandpa Cooper's in a letter to my father. My grandfather was now a Major in the Royal Artillery, based in Glasgow. He included the following fatherly advice regarding Richard's journey across London from King's Cross to Victoria, as he returned from Kingswood School, based at their temporary headquarters at Uppingham instead of the lofty site near the top of Lansdown Hill in Bath:

> By the way, don't make any casual American acquaintances while crossing London on your own. There are said to be a number of deserters and real bad hats knocking about the streets, so if anyone starts making conversation, don't get hooked in. Its a pity, because the rotters are probably only a fraction of 1%, but they are real rotters and need steering completely clear of. A word to the wise!

Family scandal

The first of two bombshells in two years hit the Browns in 1943, which really led to them moving from Lyminster to Crewkerne three years later. Nesta, husband of John Brown, and their two boys, Andrew and Stevie, returned home from America. They had travelled by ship across the Atlantic to Lisbon, and had then caught a plane to Bristol Airport. As the weeks rolled by in 1943, it became increasingly obvious that Nesta was expecting a third child. The rather large problem was that a third party was the father, and not John Brown. This not only contravened all social and moral codes of the time, but was made worse by the strict religious faith through which the Browns led their lives. Nesta and John divorced soon after the war, and he also resigned his post at Edinburgh Academy, acting over-chivalrously over the whole process. He took the blame for the whole event. The times were so different then.

The Mosquito crash

In November, a Mosquito hit the elm tree west of the cricket field, and before it could get to the front of the house it had crashed to earth and columns of flame were rising only a few yards from the ha-ha wall. Harold Endersby, the Browns' umpire-gardener, had rushed in to the house, realising the plane was in difficulty as it barely missed the tower of the church. Harold tried to get near to see if he could help – but without success. Other farm workers joined the scene including 18-year-old George Carmen who was quickly told to stay back as the two airmen were cremated in the inferno. Victor Jelly, one of a large family of gypsies who lived in a small house in Church Lane, succeeded in reaching one of the pilots and grabbed his uniform trying to extricate the airman from the burning inferno. Young Jelly pulled and pulled, but was finally beaten back by the flames and the two Mosquito airmen were cremated at the spot where they had crashed. The plane had turned a somersault, the petrol tanks bowling ahead along a cinder path. Lyminster folk today still speak of Victor Jelly's courage, stating that he deserved a decoration to commemorate his bravery.

The house was undamaged and the Guernsey herd untouched, but Annie, the Browns' ailing cook, who had been very ill, was absolutely terrified by the whole incident and died a few days later. The terror had loosened a fatal clot. The Station-Commander at Ford wrote to Vi Brown who had helped the Air Force inspection team clear up, which had included Vi picking up bits of skull from the crash, bringing home the realities of war.

The opening of a second front in Western Europe was only a matter of time away, although folk did not know for sure when the actual date would be. In the next few months, 1944 would not only bring D-Day, but a new sinister German threat – the dreaded doodle-bugs.

Chapter 21

1944 – D-Day, June 6th

Michael Blair

Michael Blair was a great friend of the Brown family . Vi Brown had got to know Michael particularly well while his parents were in India and he lived with his aunt Miss Carrie. Vi's son John was a welcome guest at the home. Michael Blair, in return, had stayed at Lyminster House in 1940 whilst on vacation from Oxford University. A gifted scholar, he won two rugby Blues and was captain of the XV in his second season. He also played for the Scottish International wartime side. A keen golfer, Michael Blair had taken Vi and Cecil Brown to Moffat Golf Course in 1941. The Browns reciprocated later in the year at the Goodwood course on the Sussex Downs.

As D-Day approached in the Lyminster area, more and more strange equipment was being lined up under the shelter of tree-lined hedgerows. Michael Blair was a Lieutenant in the Reconnaissance Corps of the XVth Scottish Division stationed in West Sussex. The Division was not part of the first assault landings and waited for the order to join the D-Day pioneers. In the early hours of June 6th, all the inhabitants of Lyminster House and Church Lane were awoken by the droning and humming of aircraft in the Sussex skies. Wave upon wave of planes and gliders launched the start of D-Day. On the evening of that 'longest' day, Michael Blair joined a large gathering of people on the lawn at Lyminster House, who had come to watch the countless reinforcements flying low to the sunset-dyed south-west sky towards the Normandy beaches, only 90 miles away. The excitement and jubilation greeting the event blurred the mind to the reality of the fate awaiting thousands of Allied troops. Nobody knew that it would be Michael's last visit to the house as he tucked into Maud Cooper's supper of freshly-laid eggs and strawberries. Taking a wireless with him to relieve the stretches of non-action in Normandy, Michael Blair walked out of the large French windows into the Sussex sunset for the last time. In late June he wrote just the once to Vi Brown from Normandy, stating:

...I think we shall find the old saying about the war being 'a period of intolerable boredom punctuated by moments of intense fear' very true indeed.

Michael Blair's death is recorded in Richard Docherty's *Only the Enemy in Front (Every other beggar behind) – The Recce Corps at War 1940–1946*. A battalion of the 43rd Wessex Division was to taken Eteville and be supported by the 9th Cameronians. The 43rd Wessex failed to take the village. Lt. Blair of 2 Troop made his way across a field and a farmyard to make contact with Canadian troops. The whole operation had been designed to take pressure off the 1st US Army by deepening the bridgehead. On July 15th, Lt. Blair was hit by a mortar bomb at his traffic point. He never recovered consciousness. Michael Blair is buried in the Ryes War Cemetery, Bazenville, Calvados in France. The cemetery is situated three kilometres to the east of the village of Sommervieu, near Bayeux. The site is not far inland from the beaches at Arromanches, where the 50th Division landed on D-Day. There are over 600 war casualties commemorated in this site.

Trifler Captain John Blake MC

On June 3rd, another great Trifler was killed in action. Captain John Blake MC was leading a troop in 43 Royal Marine Commando on an island in the Adriatic. After attending Aldenham School, where he played in the 1st XI from 1933 to 1936, scoring 502 runs in the 1935 season at an average of 41.83, he went up to Cambridge in 1937, when he played in the Freshman's match. John Blake won a Cambridge Blue in 1939, averaging a respectable 28.34 in the process and played occasionally for Hampshire from 1937 to 1939. His fielding won much praise in the 1939 University Match at Lords; he ended the innings of J. M. Lomas who was on 91, running in from the deep to take a tumbling catch. Lomas had hit 11 4s, mainly through the late cut and off drive. Ironically, Blake's catch was in response to Lomas's only lofted shot of the match. John Blake then threw down the wicket of R. B. Proud from slip, so dismissing the two most successful Oxford batsmen when each seemed set for a hundred. Proud was dismissed for 82, scoring 12 4s. Oxford declared their second innings on 273 for 3 wickets, leaving Cambridge 429 runs to win. Ending on 384, the light blues lost by 45 runs.

John Blake's brother David and father Philip had been great friends of the Triflers and skilful cricketers too. John Blake is buried in the Belgrade War Cemetery, Yugoslavia. The site is in the Uliga Baju Sekulica area of the city.

Trifler Captain John Alderson MC

Trifler John Alderson entered the army as a Lieutenant in the Seaforth Highlanders (Ross-shire Buffs, The Duke of Albany's). He had been selected for the Special Service Brigade and held the rank of Captain in No. 3 Commando. For D-Day, this Brigade comprised of Nos. 3, 4, 6 and 45 Marine Commando, totalling 24 officers and 440 other ranks divided into troops each of 3 officers and 60 men, John Alderson was one of these such officers. No. 3 Commando landed on the 'Red' area of Queen sector, 'Sword' Beach, under the direct command of Brigadier Lord Lovatt. John Alderson won the Military Cross on June 6th after his landing craft was hit by a German shell. He swam ashore and tried and get a lifeline to it.

Overall command was carried by Maj.-Gen. Gale, whom you will remember had been flown in to the Pegasus Bridge area by S. C. 'Billy' Griffith, old adversary of the Triflers. No. 4 Commando captured the gun batteries at Ouistreham and No. 6 marched inland to Benouville. Nos. 3 and 45 Commando followed these two groups as they pushed to link up with the airborne troops at Pegasus Bridge. Major Peter Young, in charge of 3 Commando remembers that:

We were in touch with 45 Commando in the Brigade's first forming up place, but progress was delayed by minefields, confining the Brigade to one track which had to be followed in single file. No. 6 Commando was ahead, but the advance was maddeningly slow.'

The Paras had captured the crucial Merville Battery in the early hours of D-Day. It was a vital target as the 75mm field guns would have wreaked havoc amongst the Allied forces. During the chaos, the Germans reoccupied the Battery. A message was passed to Major-General 'Windy' Gale that the guns were firing again. It was left to Nos. 4 and 5 Commando to retake the fortress. Unfortunately, the Germans counter-attacked again and the Commandos suffered heavy losses. The retaking of the Merville Battery caused controversy as the Commandos did not have the necessary explosives to blow the guns up. Did the guns actually start firing again? The German Commander of the Battery has stated that they did not.

John Alderson was badly wounded on D-Day +2. No. 3 Troop were attacked whilst on patrol in the Amfreville/Le Plein area. He was shot in the knee. John returned home to recuperate, but was desperate to get back to his troop and to see the crossing of the Rhine, an event which he dreamed of and the significance of which was the ultimate statement of intent in the war against Nazi Germany. The final frontier.

The British and Canadian advance from Caen was very slow and caused considerable tension between Montgomery and the Americans in particular. The Americans did not fully appreciate the fact that there were several top SS Panzer units fighting in the Caen area, including the fanatical 12th Hitlerjugend Panzers led by the notorious Kurt Meyer who was later tried and executed for the many war crimes his troops perpetrated. The Americans swept west from the Omaha and Utah before moving south and then east to Le Mans trapping the Germans in what became known as the Falaise Pocket. On August 13th, the British and Canadians attacked from Northern Normandy in order to link up with the US XVth Division. The 'Gap' was finally closed by Polish tanks, one of which stands today on top of Mt Ormel as a lasting memorial to the Battle of Normandy. The Allies took 30,000 prisoners and 10,000 German soldiers died. It took until 1961 to fully clear the battlefield. Von Kluge, the German Commander in the field, took cyanide on August 18th.

He would be followed in this act by Germany's most famous soldier, Rommel, on October 14th. Rommel had been given the option of doing so rather than being slowly executed along with the other conspirators who tried to blow up Hitler on July 20th.

The supporting Army

Grandpa Cooper had reached the rank of Major and was about to embark on the second military venture into France in 30 years since Kitchener's BEF earned the Kaiser's offensive title 'The Contemptible Army' in August 1914. My grandfather knew that this would be his chance to help liberate Europe from German aggression for a second time. His work in the supporting Company of the Royal Artillery ended up with him playing an important role in the Allied Control Commission in Hanover. Overall, his job would see him concerned with the resettlement of 'displaced persons', sorting out concentration camp survivors, dealing with collaborators and producing agricultural surveys to see how much food could be produced in the local areas where the BLA had passed through. In 1965, the newspaper *Hannoversche Allgemeine* published a series of articles on his work in the city after the war. Grandpa was known as the 'Food King', ensuring that the starving populace were properly fed.

His sense of fair play and immaculate English manners meant that he would became very popular with the local Dutch population, prior to him reaching Germany. Several lifelong friendships resulted. His War Diaries give a super insight into his experiences as he followed the fighting army through Europe. He did not always like what he saw in terms of the behaviour of the Allied Forces and was not slow to deal with the isolated incidents of looting.

There was more than a certain sense of adventure and pride in the first of his diary entries for the period from September 1944 to July 1945:

Wednesday, 13th September

Paid a batman 2/6d to wake me up at 04.30 this morning, but I woke at 03.50 on my own...

We had a sketchy lunch on board, and were soon in touch with the French coast. What we saw next was beyond what one imagined possible, but I suppose description would not be allowed (censorship). Anybody who says we muddle through should have a look at it and try to imagine how long ago the planning and manufacturing must have started. It was a great experience treading where the invasion army trod. I am really quite enjoying the experience...

Various somewhat skinny brindled Normandy cows are tethered here and there. A few sheep looking quite fat. Goodish downland country but the soil seems as though it would be very sticky indeed when wet. (800 Jerry prisoners were waiting at the quay to go back and lots more were waiting their turn.)'

Grandpa Cooper had in fact landed at Arromanches. The sight of the Mulberry harbours must have been incredible, and the thought of the D-Day invasion just a few weeks previously even more so. The name Mulberry is mistakenly attributed to the Mulberry tree which stood in the grounds of Kingswood School, Bath. The Admiralty had taken over the buildings at the start of the war, forcing Kingswood into temporary exile.

Grandpa Cooper was to pass just to the south of the Flanders battlefields where he'd fought in the Great War.

Here he was, 30 years later, probably the only member of Kitchener's 'First 250' volunteers to be involved in the 39–45 war. Occasionally, his Company would even get ahead of the main army, especially when the Germans had pushed the Allies back during the Battle of the Bulge later in 1944.

Arnhem and Trifler John Bune

On August 18th, General De Gaulle made a triumphant return to Paris as he followed the Allied troops into the French capital. The race to Berlin was seriously slowed in September when the British, ignoring several pieces of intelligence data regarding German troop movements, planned on landing paratroopers at Arnhem. Trifler John Bune was a Major in the Parachute Regiment at Arnhem. Operation Market Garden had all the ingredients of daring, risk and imagination. The failure of the plan nevertheless resulted in a permanent tie of friendship between Holland and Britain. It is possible that Montgomery was desperate to impose his personal stamp on the end of the war and silence, once and for all, American criticisms of the British performance after D-Day. Montgomery had been described by General Bradley as pious and teetotalling. Bradley was shocked at Montgomery's ambitious plan, because the British general was so cautious normally in his efforts to avoid wastage of human life. The overall strategy was based on linking the captured port of Antwerp with the Allied push through Holland, for which supplies were desperately needed. The specifics concentrated on taking the bridges over the following rivers and canals:

1. The River Rijn at Arnhem.
2. The Wilhelmina Canal, the Dommel and Willems Canal around Eindhoven.
3. The Grave bridge over the Maas.
4. The bridge over the Waal at Nijmegen.

The airborne landing took place on Sunday, September 17th, under the cover of 1,200 fighter planes. Because of a shortage of planes and gliders, three waves of aircraft were needed. This meant that the second and third waves had to be dropped in strategic places in order to support the first wave. The biggest problem for the British side of the operations centred around Arnhem, where their radios proved unsuitable for the area. This forced General Urquhart to take charge of the front line himself, making the whole process of communication with other Divisions even worse. By evening, the 2nd Battalion of the First Parachute Brigade under Lt. Col. John Frost had reached the Arnhem road bridge, but was pinned down and surrounded. One Company was three miles from the higher ground at Arnhem as the light was fading fast. Colonel Dobie sent his second in command, Major John Bune, on a reconnaissance mission in order to gain much needed information as the communications problem was badly affecting the mission. Major Bune reported back that R Company's retreat was being hindered by the need to care for the wounded. Colonel Dobie sent all the jeeps at his disposal to take the wounded to field hospitals.

Major John Bune's detachment of jeeps were ambushed by the crack troops of the 9th SS Panzer division. He was killed during the night of September 17th, 1944. On October 30th, Major Cecil Cooper (520 CA det. Corps) wrote home to Lyminster stating that John Bune was posted as missing in *The Times* and was quite likely a prisoner: unfortunately, that was never to be.

Major John Bune was killed on Sunday, September 17th, aged 30. He is buried in the Oosterbeek War Cemetery in the Netherlands, seven kilometres west of Arnhem on the road to Wagingen.

Major Cecil Cooper's letters also exchanged the news, views and the farming scene at Lyminster with his wife Linda. The atmosphere at Lyminster House itself was not happy. Nesta's predicament was the root of this feeling. Allied to that, Maud Cooper, Vi Brown's cousin and faithful servant, was 75 and almost crippled with her knee; the Asplins wanted to move and the Browns started to think the unthinkable and leave Lyminster. John Brown had resigned his post at the Edinburgh Academy as a result of Nesta's affair. He was planning to stand as a Parliamentary candidate for the Commonwealth Party. In the end, John decided to support the campaign of Sir Rodney Acland, leader of the party.

Cecil Cooper loved a good political debate. He had plenty of opportunities whilst an officer in the Army. The Russian danger particularly worried the Dutch where Cecil was based. He wrote that:

The only hope for the world and Utopia in our time is to take Russia at her word, hopefully she is altruistic, we must treat them as though they are.

November 9th, 1944

...Had agreed with one of the Burgermasters to transport a father and six children (under 7) to the town where their mother was in hospital, wounded. At Burgermaster's office was a man, wife, pram and two children. I told them to get in, thinking the size of the family exaggerated, specially as they wanted to go to same town. Then I went and saw the Burgermaster who said I'd got the wrong family! In the end I set off with 2 fathers, one mother, one helper, 8 children, one interpreter, one driver and self – about the number that used to sit down to Sunday dinner at Lyminster House. Went off down main road. Had to return and to return and take roundabout route. Reached small pontoon bridge – under repair. Asked for priority when traffic should restart, and received it from an M. P. as I was taking the kids to hospital. Just about to start up when up ran an RE (Royal Engineer) who had been working on the remains of the original bridge. All traffic must stop as he had laid a charge and was about to blow it. I spun the yarn to him too, and away we went, and reached the town (no name given). The staff I wanted had moved that morning. Deposited family at convent.

In late December, Polly and Richard Cooper received letters from Jenny and Wiesje Aghina, children of Dr Aghina who Cecil Cooper was helping in Holland. The following extracts have been taken to show the background to this doctor being helped by Cecil, above and beyond both the call of his duty and his orders:

Dear Polly,

I have seen your photograph in the office of your father. He is very busy every day. I only see him at meals and in the evening after finishing his letters to his family at home. Then he is sitting in his chair and listens to the B. B. C.

...We are dwelling in the neighbourhood of Utrecht in a little town called Amersfoort. My father is a surgeon and very hated by the Dutch Quislings. They have already put him into prison as a hostage. It was a very anxious time for my mother and us because when somebody sabotages against the Germans, then my father would be killed. After sitting two years in prison he came home at Christmas last year. It was a happy day!

...But now it is still necessary for him to hide. We have a secret place for him and when at night the bell rings, then my father dives into that place.

...Many greetings from your friend in Holland,

Jenny

Grandpa Cooper's war diaries continued to illustrate rare aspects of how the war affected ordinary civilians, caught in the front line. He was able to commandeer some penicillin for Jenny Aghina's father, a Doctor in the Dutch town of Vlijmen:

December 2nd, 1944

Went to see Dr. Aghina in hospital, he was bucked up by the idea of getting penicillin. (Later picked up three days penicillin from hospital.)
Went to Josephine Baker ENSA show this evening. Not bad, singing more than dancing.

Cecil's kindness was never forgotten, the penicillin project was not part of his job. The Aghinas later presented him with a handkerchief embroidered with the message:

FROM YOUR FRIENDS FROM VLIJMEN

My father visited the Aghinas after the war:

December 3rd, 1944

Aghinas delighted! Have invited the Coopers to Vlijmen after the war. Eventually billeted in a Belgian chateau. Owner was a diamond merchant, and is said to have made millions collaborating with the Germans. Is now in jail. I have to visit all the Burgomasters in order to keep the food supply lines running.'
After the war, the Aghinas and other Dutch families came to stay with the Browns and Coopers at Wayford Manor Farm, Crewkerne, after their move from Sussex to Somerset.

Chapter 22

1945 – VE Day and the move from Lyminster

My grandfather had the honour of representing his country at the ceremony to commemorate the liberation of Gennep. His diary entry for March 26th, 1945 outlines the day's events:

> Burgermaster of Gennep invited Major Morgan and me to represent Britain at ceremonial hoisting of flag at Town Hall. About twenty officials; cigars and cognac, and then we assembled in front. The population, some 20 Burghers had gathered, and the cheer started off with 'God Save' while we stood stiffly at the salute. Then a short speech from Burgo, more salutes while the flag went up and the Netherlands anthem was sung. Quite impressive and moving.

One year later, the Burgomaster of Gennep wrote the following letter to Cecil Cooper:

Gemeente Gennep
14/2/46

Dear Major Cooper,
On May 3rd and 4th about twenty members of the Scottish Battalion above mentioned are going to celebrate with us our liberation. The Municipality would appreciate it very much if you, who helped us so extraordinary well as an C. A. Officer, would be present then. Can you send me the address of Major Morgan?

The Burgomaster of Gennep,
[Signature unreadable!]

April 1st, 1945

Greven, Germany [name of town added after the war due to censorship]. All along the road came streams of escaped prisoners or foreign workers, giving V signs or smiling and shouting as I passed. I talked to one lot of Belgians and villainous-looking but very happy Greeks, also some Poles and many Russians.

I saw many parties of German prisoners accompanied by our boys, one or two bunches were straggling along on their own carrying white flags. Met up with some of Bobby Flood's friends [6th Airborne Division, 8th Battalion, Parachute Regiment and a Trifler, his parents were long time friends of the Coopers].

Some of the looting and pillaging by our chaps has been beyond description. This even happened while we were in Holland.

Met John Alderson today [Captain in No. 3 troop Commando, Trifler married to Cecil Cooper's niece Diana Burgin] – he drove past me in a jeep and we spotted each other, he is supposed to be coming to dinner tonight.

Busy sorting out latest batch of 'Displaced Persons' – Russians, Poles, a few Italians and some Dutchmen.

April 3rd, 1945
Found 12 Russians in a shed this morning, all dead drunk from drinking wood alcohol. They were actually dead.

April 5th, 1945
We are still getting uniformed and ununiformed surrenders. It's a queer jumble. One was a Netherlander who was found to be an SS man.

Cecil Cooper's 'right hand man' was an individual named 'George the Greek'. George had extracted the impostor's SS pay book from him. Old George was particularly adept at sniffing out an SS man from the crowd of authentic refugees.

Cecil's diaries from April 11th right through to July were sent to the German newspaper *Hannoversche Allgemeine* in 1965. The paper was commemorating the twentieth anniversary of the end of WW2. Unfortunately, this section of his diaries was never returned. The following extracts from the paper give a final picture of Major Cecil Cooper's work. By the end of the war, he was in charge of food distribution in the Hanover/West Phalia area.

Cecil's later work with the Allied Control Commission in 1945 brought him into contact with many Germans of differing views. He was quick to point out that many of the inmates of the concentration camps who he had to deal with were Germans themselves and not Nazis, and that people should avoid blindly assimilating the two as one and the same. He was keen to stay in the army after the war, hoping to apply for a post of Lt. Colonel. However, my grandmother had been running the herd and farm on her own in Sussex, and this was the main factor in him leaving the army in June 1945. Cecil was keen to make a break from the Browns: it had not always been an easy marriage with them, but finding an alternative career at the age of 51 was not going to be easy.

The Crossing of the Rhine

On March 23rd, 1945, 3,000 guns of the British 2nd Army and the US 9th Army battered the German positions over the Rhine. Amphibious tanks then crossed the river in a giant convoy. By sunrise, the Allies had secured their position across the Rhine. Winston Churchill watched the next stage in the proceedings: 2,000 aircraft dropping British and American Divisions over the Rhine. By March 26th, seven 40-ton bridges over the Rhine had been built by Allied engineers. The race to Berlin was on, thus starting, in effect, the beginnings of the Cold War between Russia and their wartime Allies, Britain and America. Only Churchill realised the extent of the Russian plans to build a metaphorical curtain of countries in Eastern Europe, thereby protecting themselves from Western influence. It was this totalitarian thinking which sent thousands of ex-Russian POWS in Germany straight through the victory parade in Moscow to forced labour camps in Siberia, infected in Stalinist eyes by capitalist influence whilst in captivity.

Wynford Vaughan-Thomas, a BBC reporter, watched as the great armies of Russia and America finally meet at Torgau. By the afternoon, he observed a makeshift fence separating the two, as both sides felt uncomfortable about further fraternisation. Vaughan-Thomas later reflected that he saw the first semblance of an Iron Curtain raised in those few hours; after the joy of uniting, the Allied armies very quickly gave way to political distrust.

The death of Trifler John Alderson

Trifler John Alderson was renowned for hitting fast bowlers back over their heads for six. Such panache, courage and daring also won him the Military Cross on D-Day. His one ambition in the war was to see the successful crossing of the Rhine: this would be more than a military operation, rather a defining statement in the whole struggle against Nazi Germany, the final act of justice.

In James Ladd's *Commandos and Rangers of World War 2,* the story of John Alderson's 3 Marine Commando Troop is well recorded. Crossing the Rhine in LVTs, passing through the leading 1 Commando, they cleared the town of Wesel with 46 Royal Marine Commandos and 45 Royal Marine Commandos. On April 3rd, 3 Commando marched for 19 hours before attacking Osnabruck from high ground in the north-west, the Germans surrendering the following day. The officers of 3 Commando made a base at a local mansion, while the men found a brewery to sleep in overnight!

They then followed 6 Commando across the river Weser. Their target was to be the V2 rocket factory near the town of Leese. On April 8th, Captain John Alderson was sitting next to his commanding officer, Lt. Col. Bartholomew in a light tank, when he was hit by a single sniper's bullet. John Alderson is buried in the Rheinberg War Cemetery 24 kilometres north of Krefeld and 13 kilometres south of the town of Rheinberg on the road to Kamp Lintfort. The site of the cemetery was chosen in April 1946 by the Army Graves Service for the assembly of British and Commonwealth graves recovered from the numerous German cemeteries in the area.

News of John Alderson's death shattered all folk at Lyminster – to Vi Brown he had been a second son. His death left his widow Diana (née Burgin) with three young children, Judith, Phillippa and Christopher.

Hanover

In Germany, there was a mountain of work to do after the fighting army had done their job. My grandfather's role in the Allied Control Commission basically took the form of developing a Military Government in the newly conquered towns and cities. As previously mentioned, the *Hannoversche Allgemeine* published a series of articles from his diaries in 1965, but unfortunately did not return the entries from April 11th to July. The article makes for fascinating reading. I had a rather rose-coloured picture of the Allies simply moving into Germany and everything being sorted out in a glorious moral mission where the refugees and newly liberated POWs responded in a measured and balanced way. This naivety ignores the sheer chaos of the scene, which was repeated in towns and cities throughout Germany. The whole of Europe was like a gigantic crossroads of pushing prams and creaking carts, Norwegians going north and Slavs trekking south; POWs, slave labourers, concentration camp survivors – all were seeking their homes.

On April 11th, 1945, my grandfather described Hanover as being like an open wound. People were in a bemused state and couldn't grasp what was happening. General Lohning, the Commandant of Ahlem Concentration Camp, had surrendered to the Allies and was driven away to a POW camp in Hattingen. There were 60,000 foreigners, newly set free, from about 20 countries, and nothing was functioning in the city. Nobody was safe in Hanover in April 1945, not even the Allied troops. Grandpa Cooper was nicknamed the 'Food King'. The *Hanoversche Allgemeine* quoted from his diaries as follows:

For everyone who is bold enough there are more than enough problems to solve. Here are just a few of the things that happen every day:-

1. Yanks still confiscating bicycles, e. g. those of the German Civil servants, too, who work for my food department and who have a bicycle permit.

2. Russians, armed with hand grenades, robbed two of my lorries that I use to transport food, ripped off the military government ID plates and injured five people (Germans). But the Americans are responsible for the Russians.

On May 7th, he wrote:

We have spoken to other officers about the Russians looting and their general behaviour in Hanover. They are without doubt a threat to the population. The French, Belgians and Dutch have generally behaved well, the Poles and Russians not. But when we consider what the Germans did in Russia and what the British, Canadian and Allied soldiers got up to in Holland, which suffered both at the hands of its enemies as well as its friends, then one should be more careful with remarks that the Russians, and particularly these here after years of forced labour, are all barbarians.

Two Poles, Tadek and Dabravska, had set up their own form of Nuremberg Trial scenario in the Town Hall. People were beaten and it was turning into a kangaroo court and concentration camp. Grandpa Cooper registered 54,000 displaced persons in Hanover for his daily rations transport. There was a particularly high percentage of slave labourers in Hanover: 38 per cent of the total work force was foreign. Attacks on Germans by foreigners peaked just after the Occupation troops marched in and when rumours of mass graves caused fear at the end of April. SS men shot 250 people on April 8th and buried them at Seelhurst. The graves were opened and the bodies were interned separately behind the town hall. Of these poor folk, 154 were shot in the back of the neck. A further 69 slaves died of exhaustion. From a second grave, 303 bodies were exhumed, probably killed three months before. Apart from a few Frenchmen, the majority of the victims were either Russians or Slavs. Researching this aspect of the war was particularly disturbing. My grandfather saw all the hell of the camp at Ahlem, and this wasn't a large extermination camp either, like the one at Auschwitz. Even when faced with the background of the freshly exhumed bodies, he was desperate for the conquering forces to be as morally spotless, hence his referral to Allied looting in Holland.

The Germans knew that the war would be shortly over, but still the SS continued to murder, violently committed to their abhorrent ideology right up to the end of the war, which the majority of Germans had supported in voting for Hitler in 1933. They were silent supporters of the murder of innocent people by the SS. Hitler's racial theories, regarding the Jew and the Slav as inferior, had been clearly laid out in *Mein Kampf*. The SS were the cultural icons for a people who believed that the Ayran race were superior in every way. And yet my grandfather clearly saw that not all Germans supported Hitler; remember there were many who languished in the camps as well.

Throughout Europe on VE Day, a mass of refugees formed a huge army of its own, thousands of displaced persons returning to their homes if they still had one. The whole of Europe was on the march. Some folk were rapidly travelling west in order to avoid the Russians. Feeding the thousands and thousands of refugees, ex-slave labourers and displaced persons was an incredible feat. It took place against a background of understandable open revenge, violence, mayhem and sabotage. The effectiveness of my grandfather's work and his desire to see fair play is something to hand on to posterity.

In Britain, enormous celebrations broke out in every village, town and city. For those families who had lost loved ones, the parties reflected those who would never come back, a grey sombre mood amidst joyous cheering and merrymaking. Grandpa Cooper's thoughts turned back to November 1918 and the last Armistice. He had been with the Royal East Kents (The Buffs) stranded in remote Salonica, hundreds of miles away from the Western Front where he had taken part in almost every battle in the 1914–18 campaign. Just after VE Day, Cecil wrote to his son Richard, boarding at Kingswood School. The poignant comments contained in these extracts are good advice to all those folk who think that there is always something else better going during times of celebration:

Maj. C.C. Cooper,
229 (D) Mil. Gov. Det.
B. L. A.
14–5–1945

My Dear Rich,

Many thanks for your V. E. Day thoughts. Don't be too disappointed that the day came and went with a feeling of empty sausageness as its main characteristic. I'm no pessimist, but that is frequently the case with an event however prodigious that one really had confidence would come about somehow, sometime.

One naturally feels that one has missed something – if at home by not being with ones contemporaries and if away, by not being at home. I always feel that I was robbed of the last Armistice because I did not join in the mob emotions of the chaps riding on top of taxi cabs and waving flags until they fell off. This time I sat in my bedroom and wrote to my family.

Don't mistake me – nothing would be more natural

than of feeling that you could do more justice to the occasion if you were elsewhere, but even if you had been elsewhere you would either have felt the exuberance was pretty artificial or that it would have been a lot better somewhere else.

Is this pessimistic? I don't believe so, but I'm not dogmatic about it. Tell me if you think it is. It does not mean that there is no joy in achievement. Perhaps it means that there is more happiness in effort than result.

...I want my family and home but the opportunities here are somewhat larger than in a small farm and what is more I get well paid for doing something that I find highly interesting.

Lots of love and keep your chin up.
Always yours in joy and despondency.

Dad.

It was time for the Browns to leave Lyminster House behind, the end of the war being an apt moment in time. The Coopers had to decide whether or not to remain with them. Cecil Cooper returned home in late June 1945, his love of army life to be put into second place as he placed family before his own ambition.

Sir Michael Woodruff

Good family news arrived from Changi Gaol in August. Vi Brown and Cecil Cooper's oldest nephew, Michael Woodruff, found himself showered with leaflets dropped from an American Liberator bomber explaining that Japan had unconditionally surrendered. On September 3rd, 1945, the Union flag once again flew over Changi. Michael Woodruff's job now was to get the information gathered in Changi about deficiency diseases as quickly as possible to his friend Professor R. D. (later Sir Douglas) Wright. Michael had saved hundreds of lives. His father,

Professor Harold Woodruff, came to meet his son at Essendon Airport, Melbourne, avoiding the emotional stress of coming back by boat to thousands of waiting Australians at Port Melbourne. It was a good fifteen minutes though before father and son could speak, such was the intensity of the moment.

Another Cooper cousin was not so lucky: although he survived the Japanese camps for some years, he never regained full health. Douglas Brumley was the husband of Atholl Cooper's daughter Betty. Atholl, the brother of Vi Brown and Cecil Cooper, had remained in Australia since 1913.

VE Day came and went, but the scene at Lyminster would never be the same. Standing on the ha-ha in the summer of 1945 was a sad affair. The cricket ground remained in its wartime state. The outfield lay overgrown, long grasses billowed in the warm summer breezes, the last decade seemed an eternity away. No more cricket was ever played at Lyminster House. Many cricketers who graced the wonderful ground would never come back, perishing in the war. People like Edmund Symes-Thompson, the jolliest of raconteurs – life was never dull when he was present. John Alderson, who had lived with the Browns in the 30s, inseparable from his puffing pipe, was missed more than any other. It was the end of an era as England itself moved into the post-war period.

For Aunt Vi Brown, it signified the end of a dream, a dream where cricket had represented values to the greater good. A social system where money permeated throughout those who had contact with the Browns, both family and workers. Before the cry of 'patronisation' is heard, the large country houses of the new millennium are inhabited by the icons of the pop and football world. They have no sense of duty toward their fellows, no sense of tradition or Englishness. They exist only to wallow in the crass wealth gained largely through the gullibility of modern England.

Would it be so outrageous to suggest that rural communities were far happier in the old class regime? Perhaps. At least they were exactly that though – communities. Not lines of houses with cars outside, ready to escape to the nearest haven of the town supermarket, the village post office, shop and pub having closed.

Chapter 23

1946 - Wayford Manor Farm, Crewkerne

1947 Captain Richard Cooper RASC outside 'Nyarrin', Wayford, nr Crewkerne.

In October 1946, the Browns and Coopers upped and moved to Somerset, buying Wayford Manor Farm. The partnership continued as Cecil Brown also decided to retire from Lloyds of London. They left behind a piece of Sussex which would never be quite the same again. Wayford Manor Farm, near Crewkerne, lies just inside the county of Somerset, a few miles from the Dorset border. The first task was to recondition five cottages for the farmworkers, build two new ones, and a new detached bungalow where Major Cecil and Linda Cooper would live. The farm was positioned on hilly land between 300 and 700 above sea level. The house was situated on a mini-plateau overlooking the Axe valley. Across this valley lay a thousand fields, a patchwork quilt of differing shades of green. In the distance, softly wooded Lewsden and the bleak escarpment of Pilsden Pen formed twin mini-peaks, regimentally guarding the soft countryside. The latter hill at 909 is the highest point in Dorset.

The Guernsey herd followed the Browns and Coopers to Somerset too. The farm was much larger than the one at Lyminster. Unfortunately, the cows did not take too kindly to their new move. In the first year coughs and bronchitis led to eight of them dying. Pedigree cows were more delicate than crossbreeds, and an importation of new cows from the Channel Islands had brought in the infection. It was difficult to accept, though, that an attested herd which had moved to an attested farm could meet with so much bad luck. At first it was thought that that the muddy farmyard had caused the problem. It hurt Vi and Cecil Cooper to see the herd knee-deep in squelchy mud. Animal welfare isn't quite such a new phenomenon, you see. The yard was covered with concrete as soon as possible.

Summer 1947. Our Guernsey herd, Wayford Manor Farm nr Crewkerne. Lewsdon Hill and Pilsden Pen (909') in the distance.

Many of the cows were Championship winners at the Channel Islands sections of local agricultural shows. Old Linda's Pride and Polly's Pride were two such animals, named after Linda and Polly Cooper. When a new cow joined the herd, Vi Brown likened it to a gaggle of lady members of a golf club inspecting a stranger. Nervous cows never let their milk down.

Within a few months, the hard winter of 1947 added its own chapter of hardship to the period of post-war austerity. Vi Brown records that from January 29th to March 5th, the snow drifts lay thick and fast.

Lyminster seemed a long way away. Vi, though, continued to act with the local community's best interests at heart. She gave local children their own garden at Wayford in response to them indiscriminately picking hedgerow flowers. Their own play area in one of the fields was soon added. Linda Cooper took the wives of the farmworkers to the shops in Crewkerne once a week in the Daimler Vi also became a governor of Clapton Primary School a mile away; however, she was too forward thinking for the other members. Vi quickly was viewed as a dissident on such a conservative body and resigned.

The Browns acted quickly to provide a cricket net for use by the sons of old Triflers who came to stay in the holidays. John Brown took boys on tour to the West Country from Emmanuel School in London, his first post after resigning from the Edinburgh Academy as a result of his divorce from Nesta. Such over-chivalrous behaviour would be mocked today.

Vi Brown also busied herself with a number of new community projects. These included starting the Women's Institute and the Clapton Flower Show where the Lyminster Cup is still awarded to the present day. Both projects were great successes. An attempt to initiate a local play-reading circle failed though.

Many visitors came to see the Browns from all over the world. Wayford would never see such a diverse range of people visit the sleepy hamlet again. The farmhouse became an outpost of rich cosmopolitan culture. From the Federation of University Women came Andree, a French graduate struggling for health after years in a Nazi concentration camp. Two Norwegians followed her, Eva and Astrid, both of whom had been active in their country's resistance movement. Old American friends, Margaret Corman and Barbara Cohen, visited in 1953 as part of their trip to see the Coronation. Margaret then sent other guests – Dr. Pettingill, Professor of Economics, and Miss Mathews of Kentucky, teacher of English and lover of literature. Many old Triflers and Australian Cooper relations enjoyed the traditional Brown hospitality at Wayford. These included Michael Woodruff's brother Pip, Director of Public Health in South Australia, Michael's father-in-law Keith Ashby, and his daughter Beth. The Ashbys were great Quakers, and Vi Brown was rapidly moving towards their beliefs:

I felt a kinship with my own slowly, and at times truculently, worked out beliefs, which have made me feel so often a misfit in the company of the orthodox.

1953 Reunion From Left: Uncle Cecil " CNB" Brown, Auntie Brenda Cooper,
Auntie Elsie Holmes (née Cooper) at Wayford Manor Farm

She would have a Quaker funeral in 1970. Her beliefs were also influenced by reading Paul Cadbury's article, written soon after his visit to Russia in the early 50s.

In 1953, Elsie Holmes (née Cooper) and Atholl Cooper (married to Dorothy Holmes, sister of Elsie's husband), came to England from Australia for what was really the last time that the brothers and sisters of Vi and Cecil Cooper came together for a reunion, never to be repeated again.

The old influence of Vi's education at the famous North London Collegiate School for Girls was rekindled when Edith Cross came to stay. She had organised the NLCSG Archives display for the school's centenary in 1951. The school was perhaps many, many years ahead of its time. At the turn of the century, it educated hundreds of girls for university. The school also practised a policy of religious tolerance, not a common thing in the top schools of the early 20's where they tended to be very denominational in character. Vi planted an oak, beech and pine wood at Pyre Cross at Wayford. It was named Drummondswood after Miss Drummond, Headmistress of the NLCSG and her niece Ruth, a great friend of Vi's sister Brenda.

Wayford had never seen such a time in its history or since in terms of being a meeting place for so many folk from across the world. A trip to the Blue Boy a mile down the road in Clapton was the furthest that many local people had got in their lives.

Vi and Cecil Brown retired to Bradford Road, Sherborne in 1953. The eastern part of Manor Farm was given to Cecil and Linda Cooper, who went into partnership with my parents Richard and Margaret Cooper. The Manor Farmhouse, the rest of the farm, the bungalow and three cottages went for the princely sum of £15,000.

Grandpa Cooper had now been put in the position where for the first time in 30-odd years he had a chance to enjoy real farming success. The Coopers ran Lyminster Farm at Woolminstone, just a mile east of Wayford, the Guernsey herd from Sussex days went with them. Grandpa though was to suffer a cerebral stroke in 1950 – his long and arduous life was catching up with him. He still was desperate to make one last farming decision which would result in real money being made. In 1958, Landrace pigs were bought to supplement the income brought in by the Guernseys, but within a few years they had all died of disease. In 1961, Cecil and Linda retired from farming and moved from their cottage next to their son and daughter-in-law to sheltered accommodation at Combe St Nicholas near Chard.

Lyminster Farm was a small, happy dairy establishment, not really organised on intensive lines. The hedges remained intact and the birds sang. Thickets and ponds lay in corners of fields, untouched by human hand. The herd brought in a moderate income, but the riches came from living in the heart of the Somerset countryside. Richard and Margaret Cooper enjoyed the fruits of a simple rural life. The peace of walking across the land was not really quantifiable – no price could be placed on things like that.

Early in December 1967, my father became very ill, due probably to a kick in the stomach from one of the less friendly Guernseys months earlier. The intense pain he suffered was not diagnosed by local doctors. By the time he was taken to hospital nearly three weeks later, it was too late and gangrene had set in, destroying his liver. He died on Christmas Eve, 1967. Richard had been due to take part in the annual nativity play at the Methodist Church in Crewkerne. At his Memorial Service, that same church saw many of the old family from Lyminster days present. My father's dream of farming, born out of long summer days in Sussex, hay-making accompanied by the donkey cart, old Harold Endersby, sister Polly, friend John Flood and a host of visiting servicemen, had ended.

The buildings at Lyminster Farm, Woolminstone, slowly fell into ruin. The cows were quickly sold and the land rented to other farmers as grass keep. Our faithful springer spaniel, Psyche, would always walk to the old cow sheds at milking times, morning and night for years on end, waiting for the Guernseys to come into the yard. They never did. In 1978, the farm was finally sold and my mother went to live in nearby Crewkerne. Today, the farm barns have been converted into living accommodation.

What of Lyminster in Sussex? The Brown's house had been bought by Air Chief Marshall Sir William Geoffrey Salmond in 1946. He had been mentioned in despatches an incredible five times in the First World War, gaining the DSO, CMG, Legion of Honour, and the Croix de Guerre. Salmond was appointed Chief of the Air Staff in 1930, before being appointed Chief of Air Defence in 1933. Their daughter Rosemary married Nicholas Mosley, son of Sir Oswald Mosley and Lady Cynthia Blanche née Curzon. Nicholas and Rosemary were given the house 'on loan' in 1951. It was fully transferred into full ownership in the late 1950s. Nicholas Mosley became Lord Ravensdale in 1966. He remembers Lyminster House as

...the perfect family home.

The Mosleys never kept the cricket field, letting it out to a market gardener who lived in the old cricket pavilion. The tradition of cricket in the village was maintained by Bill Rice who lived at Lyminster Court, 400 yards to the north on the A284. The Rice's Brookfield ground was used to hold matches involving his friends from London.

Nicholas Mosley was churchwarden in the early 1960s, a post now held by the Brown's old cowman, George Carmen and in the more recent past by Rosemary Anne Sisson. The Church Fete was always held in the gardens of Lyminster House in the 60s and the Mosleys became great friends with most of the villagers. In 1968 they decided that the house and gardens were far too big for their needs. They sold the property to a Cockney businessman by the name of Mr Gasteen, the social and intellectual antithesis of the Browns, Salmonds and Mosleys. Gasteen kept his washing machine in the billiard room, where it continually leaked over the polished oak floor laid by Cecil Brown. Cigarette butts were left to burn scorch marks in the wooden mantelpieces. The motto of 'I am what I earn' could never have been more accurate. There was no sense of history, community or duty towards one's fellow man. Waking up late in the morning, still in pyjamas, he often used to greet visitors with 'Eff off!' The era of the Gasteen charm school thankfully ended in 1977 when he sold the western half of the house to Major-General Ronnie and Judith Buckland who restored a sense of dignity and community. As previously mentioned, Judith is famous for starting the Arundel Festival in the mid-80s. It is now a highly esteemed event with a European standing. Judith's ceaseless energy and enthusiastic determination has ensured its success. Ronnie Buckland's distinguished career in the British Army culminated in him becoming I/C Administration, UK Land Forces before retiring in 1975. He was Chief Executive of Adur District Council from 1975 to 1985. The eastern half of the house was bought by a Mr Wright, an interior designer. He then sold up and his half was further divided into two. Mr Pallis, a Greek psychologist lives in the north-eastern section with his family, and Mr Gibb, a retired accountant lives in the old servants' quarters section of the old house.

Great Aunt VI had a vision in 1931, a utopian dream which combined such diverse themes as cricket, philanthropy and the arts. It was a cocktail of divergent beliefs which established Lyminster House as a very special place, unique perhaps in the social history of the Twentieth Century. One thing for sure though is that her legacy will live on, epitomised in the final line of her autobiographical "The Silver Cord". It simply reads, "To the future I send my love." Her Fabian ideals never included the empowerment of the ignorant in society though.

Lyminster has changed like all other villages, reflecting the urbanisation of rural life which has destroyed close-knit communities. The class system has withered, only to be replaced by a crass meritocracy, more aware of wealth and materialism than its predecessor ever was. Tourists still flock to see the results of our ancestors efforts in creating the countryside we are trying hard to destroy. Hardships are few and far between now, but a self-indulgent society never really appreciates the spoils won by its forefathers. We fought a long and noble war against tyranny, Parliament was saved from the Reich.

Today, the truth is manipulated by folk who espouse freedom, but hide behind the spin of Millbank. Presidential photo shoot opportunities replacing the front bench of the Commons. The move towards a post-democratic society is underway - the complete irony. Before democracy goes the same way as the countryside, reflect on the 1930s Lyminster memories of Rosemary Anne Sisson in her wonderful book "Rosemary for Remembrance."

There are no more minnows or sticklebacks, tadpolesor newts. The streams are clogged or vanished and the water cress beds and the Knucker Hole are fenced-off and turned into a trout farm, and the cart horses replaced by tractors. We children, sleeping under thatch in unheated bedrooms, fetching milk in tin cans from the farm and running barefoot in the fields were the last of the truly privileged. And yet I know that carefree country childhood, surrounded by love and beauty, armed and strengthened us for all that was to come."

Lyminster Farm, Crewkerne was my carefree country childhood, a way of life which has disappeared.

Chapter 24

The Triflers' Cricket Club: 1932–1940

John Alderson MC: Westminster School; Lloyd's of London 1933–39; Captain No. 3 Commando; Military Cross; wounded D-Day+2; killed Leese, April 8th, 1945.

Eric Bompas: son of Cecil Henry Bompas, Indian Civil Service. Westminster School; Hong Kong and Shanghai Bank; journalist on *Oxford Mail*; 1st Mountain Battery Hong Kong and Singapore RA. Killed in action on reconnaissance behind enemy lines; posthumously mentioned in despatches, April 1946.

Michael Broadhurst: Westminster School. Major in 4th Bombay Grenadiers. Worked with Unilever and Wood.

John Stephen Brown: Westminster School; Trinity College, Cambridge. English Master, Edinburgh Academy and Emmanuel School; Captain, Royal Scots Regiment 1941–45; Headmaster, Bexhill Grammar School, 1952–68. Died 1968.

John Bune: Westminster School; St Catherine's College, Cambridge; Royal Fusiliers; then Major in the Parachute Regiment. Killed at Arnhem, September 17th, 1944.

Alan Campbell-Johnson OBE, CIE: Westminster School; Christ Church, Oxford. Press attache to Lord Mountbatten during the Partition of India. Author of *Growing Opinions* (1935); *Peace Offering* (1936); *Anthony Eden* (1938); *Viscount Halifax* (1941); *Mission* *with Mountbatten* (1951). Died January, 1998.

Charles Cecil Cooper: Fixture secretary/organiser at Lyminster. WW1 – 2nd Lieutenant, 1st Buffs (East Kent Regiment); WW2 – Major, Royal Artillery. Died January 1973.

Anthony Craxton MVO, CVO: St George's Choir School, Windsor; Royal Academy of Music and Gordonstoun School. Joined the BBC in 1941. I/C coverage of the first live Test Matches and other Outside Broadcasts. Covered Royal weddings and produced first Royal Documentary in 1967.

Sir Richard Doll: Westminster School; St Thomas's Medical School, London. OBE 1956. Kt. 1971. RAMC during WW2. Surgeon, first person to prove the link between cancer and smoking. Still working on medical research projects.

Robin Edgar: Westminster School; Christ Church, Oxford. HM Colonial Service in Nigeria. Died of yellow fever on October 15th, 1938.

John Rudd Cecil Engleheart: Westminster School. Concert pianist and conductor. Chairman and Artistic Director of the Orchestra da Camera from 1965 to 1985.

'Dick' Evers: Master at Fettes College; killed in North Africa when his jeep ran over a land mine.

Brigadier G. Robert 'Bobby' Flood: Lancing College; Reading University. 6th Armoured Division, 8th Battalion of the Parachute Regiment; served at Arnhem; became Deputy Head of Sandhurst.

Ralph Neville Heaton CB: Westminster School, Christ Church, Oxford. Deputy Secretary, Education Department under 'Rab' Butler, during which time the 1944 Education Act was produced.

Donald Knight: Two test matches for England. Played for Surrey. Master i/c Cricket at Westminster School

Rt. Hon. Sir John Brinsmead Latey: Westminster School; Christ Church, Oxford. High Court Judge. Kt. 1965.

Major General Errol Henry Lonsdale MBE, CB: Westminster School; St Catherine's College, Cambridge; RASC in WW2; AA and QMG, War Office 1951–53; ADC to the Queen 1964–66; President of the Modern Pentathlon and Biathlon 1976–80; Chairman, Institute of Advanced Motorists 1971–74.

Sir Dermot Milman: 8th Baronet. Uppingham; Corpus Christi, Oxford. Played for the England Rugby team 1937–38 (four caps); Major in the RASC; Diplomat in the British Council Overseas.

Ian Keith Munro: Westminster School; Pembroke College, Cambridge; International skier; Captain in the Royal Artillery; Devon farmer.

Francis Pagan: Westminster School; Trinity College, Cambridge. Schoolmaster, King Edward V1 School, Spilsby 1935–37; Epsom College 1937–41; Lieutenant in the RNVR in the Atlantic and Mediterranean Convoys and US Pacific Fleet. Mentioned in despatches, (N. Atlantic) May 1944; Head of Classics and Housemaster Epsom College 1946–64; PRO, Slimbridge Wildfowl Trust. Author of *Companion's Guide to Burgundy*, *Companion's Guide to the Greek Islands*.

John Owen Home Powell-Jones: Westminster School; Shell, Addis Ababa; Major in the Derbyshire Yeomanry and Somaliland Camel Corps; National Trust Official. Died September 7th, 1978.

Hon. Findlay Rea: Westminster School; organised all the competitions in the *Cricketer* magazine.

John 'Jack' Rich, MBE: Westminster School; Magdelene College, Oxford. I/C Children's Programmes at the BBC.

Lord Rodney Smith, KBE: Westminster School; St,

Thomas's Hospital, London. A famous surgeon. President of the Royal College of Surgeons. Life Peer 1978. Died 1998.

Rt. Hon. Sir John Dexter Stocker MC, TDPC: Westminster; London University. Lord Chief Justice of Appeal, 1986–92.

Arthur Collwyn Sturge, MC: Harrow School; Brasenose College, Oxford. Chairman A. L. Sturge and Co. Chairman of Lloyds of London 1970–75. (Cecil Norman Brown worked as an underwriter at A. L. Sturge.)

Edmund Symes-Thompson: Radley School; read medicine at Cambridge University; fourth generation of devoted doctors; St George's Hospital; St Luke's Hospital, Chelsea. Killed by a direct hit on Sunday, May 11th, 1941 while carrying out a blood transfusion.

John Triggs, MBE: Westminster School; Christ Church, Oxford. Major in the Border Regiment (despatches, NW Europe, March 1945); Publicity Officer, National Coal Board 1948; Chief Executive, PR Dept. Festival of Britain 1948–51.

J. F. Turner: Westminster School. Played for the MCC as well as the Triflers.

Eminent cricketers who played against the Triflers at Lyminster

C. Oakes: Sussex CCC.

J. Oakes: Sussex CCC.

'J. K. ' Mathews: Sussex CCC.

S. C. 'Billy' Griffith: England; Sussex CCC; Sec. MCC.

Hugh Bartlett: Full MCC tour; Sussex CCC.(An occasional Trifler)

Ted Bowley: Sussex CCC. (An occasional Trifler)

Lord Ebbisham: House of Commons and Lords XI and member of Ashtead CC in the 1930s.

Rev. G. L. O. Jessop: Oxford University CC.

Jack Eaton: Sussex CCC.
Rev. F. W. Gilligan Sussex CCC
J. P. Parker: Hampshire CCC.
Claude Taylor: Oxford University and Leicestershire.
A. C. (Jack) Russell: Essex and England.

Index

A

Abbey Manor Building Society 14
Ackland, Sir Rodney [Commonwealth Party] 211
Acroma [Libya, WW2] 188
Admiralty 184, 208
Adur District Council 234
Aghina family [Holland] 212, 213
Ahlem Concentration Camp, nr. Hanover 219
Aisne [Battle of] 29
Aldenham School 204
Alderson MC, John [Triflers' CC] 52, 55, 85-87, 99, 107, 113, 114, 124, 138-140, 163, 205-206, 215, 217, 218, 224
Alley, Bill [New South Wales CC, Somerset CCC and Test Match umpire] 4
Allied Control Commission 4, 10, 28, 207, 216, 219
Allied looting in Holland 215, 221
Amberley Castle 26, 169, 170
American Army 196-199, 203, 217
Amersfoot [Holland] 212
Amfreville [D+2 Day] 206
Amiss Denis [cricketer] 135
Angelo Bobby [Trifler] 52, 55
Angermering 170
Antwerp 209
Archbishop of Canterbury 27
Argos [Australian newspaper] 35
Armistice 160, 222
Armstrong, Warwick [Australian cricket team] 115
A. R. P. [Air Raid Protection] 169, 171, 184
Arnhem 4, 106, 209-211

Arromanches [Mulberry Harbours] 204, 208
Arundel 21, 25, 112, 124, 172
Arundel Arts Festival 162, 234
Arundel Castle 23, 78, 90, 95, 174
Ashby family [parents of Lady Woodruff] 230
Ashtead C. C. 63, 150, 174, 177
Asplin family [Lyminster] 45, 46, 77, 80, 97, 121, 211
Auschwitz 221
Australia 2, 12, 13, 28, 32-35, 38-41, 60-61, 93, 131, 135, 136, 146, 166, 167, 186-188, 194, 229
Australian Army 186, 187
Australian Brown snake 39

B

Bader, Douglas 17
Baldwin, Stanley [British Prime Minister] 110
Baker, Josephine[ENSA] 213
Baliol-Scott, Ursel [Triflers' CC] 83
Balkans 11
Bannister, Sir Roger 22
Barrett, Capt. RN [Trifler] 112, 126, 138, 141, 191
Bartholomew, Lt. Col. [3 Commando] 218
Bartlett, Hugh [Sussex CCC, MCC, Triflers CC] 85, 105
Bates, P. C. 123, 126, 127, 137
Battle of the Bulge 209
Battle of Britain 23, 163,168, 171, 174
Bazenville [Battle of Normandy] 203
Bayeux [D Day] 203
BBC 158, 212
Bedford RFC 146
Belgrade War Cemetery 204
Benouville [D Day] 205
Beresford, Frank [artist] 42
Berkshire Regiment 130

Berlin 58, 110, 111, 178, 217
Berlin Olympics [1936] 1, 8, 110, 178
Berwick CC 113, 140, 148
Big Bertha [WW1 gun] 74
Biggin Hill [RAF] 174
Bishop, Mr. [Lyminster] 162
Bismark [battleship] 53
Blackburn Shark aircraft 173
Blair, Lt. Michael [Oxford Rugby Blue & Scottish Wartime XV] 202, 203
Blair, Herbie [Solicitor] 60, 61, 136
Blair, P. C. [Scottish cricketer] 114
Blake family [Havant CC] 66, 67, 141, 204
Blake MC, Capt. John [Triflers' CC, Havant CC and Cambridge University CC] 66, 67, 107, 142, 158, 204
Blanche, Lady Cynthia 233
Blessed, Bill [Lyminster] 101, 171
Bletchley Park [Station X] 175
Blitz 14
Blitzkreig 171
Blossom Time [Edwardian musical] 92
Boat Race 1
Bodyline Tour [1933] 132, 135
Bognor Regis CC 67, 74, 85, 105, 106, 145, 156, 158
Bompas, Lt. Eric [Trifler] 52, 55, 185
Bowley, Ted [Sussex CCC] 66, 67
Boycott, Geoffrey 135
Bradley, Gen. Omar 209
Bradman, Don [Australian cricket team] 132
Breach, Chris [Steyning CC] 65
Brickhill, Paul "Reach for the Sky" 14
Bristol Grammar School 48
British Expeditionary Force [WW1] 164
Brittanic SS 166
Broadley, Jack [Slinfold CC] 150

Brookfield Cricket Ground, Lyminster 233
Broadhurst, Michael [Trifler] 52, 54, 55, 75
Brown, Andrew 90, 118, 166, 199
Brown, Audrey [1936 Olympic Silver medallist] 8, 111
Brown, Cecil ['CNB'] 1, 2, 12-15, 19, 26, 32, 36-38, 41-49, 53, 54, 59, 68, 90, 97, 103, 111-113, 118-122, 141, 143, 153, 156, 160, 168, 169, 172, 180, 184, 195, 211, 226, 227, 229-231
"Brown's House" 22
Brown, John ['JSB'] 19, 24, 37, 52-56, 65, 68, 85, 88-90, 108, 112, 114, 124, 156, 166, 199, 202, 210, 229, 230
Brown, Rev. J. M. 46
Brown, Vi [nee' Cooper] 1, 2, 10, 12, 15, 19, 22, 25-27, 32, 36-38, 41-49, 54, 58, 59, 64, 67, 72-82, 90, 92, 93, 95, 97, 103, 104, 109, 111-113, 118-121, 127- 129, 135, 138, 141, 142, 150, 156, 158-160, 163, 166-170, 178-180, 184-186, 189-200, 202, 203, 211,223, 227-231, 234
Brown, Godfrey [Olympic Gold medallist, Headmaster of Worcester Royal Grammar School] 8, 111
Brown, Leonard 111
Brown, Nesta [nee Clement-Jones] 87-90, 118, 166, 199, 210, 219
Brown, Sir Ralph Kilner 8, 48, 111
Brown, Stevie 166, 199
Brownshirts [Nazi] 71
Bruce-Lockheart, R. B. [Scottish Rugby International] 114
Brumley, Betty [nee Cooper] 224
Brumley, Douglas 224
Bryant, Sophie [Headmistress of the North London Collegiate School] 14, 15
Buchenwald Concentration Camp 123
Buckland, Maj. Gen. Ronnie 22, 92, 162, 234
Buckland, Judith 22, 92, 163, 234
Budd Q. C. , Bernhard 99
Buffs, The 31

Bulwinkle, Sister [Singapore massacre] 188
Bundrett, F [Havant CC] 107
Bune, John [Trifler] 52, 55, 63, 85, 86, 209-211
Burgin family 15, 21, 83, 89, 91, 99, 100, 138, 141, 151-155, 215, 218
Burgin, Rt. Hon. Leslie 13, 83, 89, 138, 141, 143, 146, 151-155, 164
Butler, Rt. Hon. Rab [Sec. of State for Ed.] 126
Byrne, Capt. RN 135
Byrne, Daphne 10, 43, 47, 135, 195
Bystander Trophy [golf] 46

C

Cadbury family 26, 230
Caen [WW2] 206
Cairo 65
Calvados [WW2] 203
Cambridgeshire CCC 67
Cambridge University 8, 26, 37, 46, 55, 67, 102, 107, 114, 115, 135, 195, 204
Cameron Highlanders of Ottawa 92, 189
Cameronians, 9th [WW2] 203
Campbell-Johnson, Alan O.B.E. C.I.E. 51-54, 56, 65, 67-73, 76, 84, 85, 135, 175
Canada 33, 184, 185, 188, 189, 191-194, 198, 203
Canadian Black Watch 180, 181, 188, 189
Canterbury Cathedral 11
Cardo, Miss [Lyminster ARP] 169, 171, 173
Carmen, George [Lyminster] 42, 101, 171, 200, 233
Carolinas, U. S. A. 112, 196
Cassel Kemmock [Belgium WW1] 29
Catholicism 11
"Cato" [Michael Foot et al] 154
Cavalry, 2nd Division [WW1] 31

Cazelet, Victor 70
Chamberlain, Rt. Hon. Nevil 1, 2, 13, 110, 123, 142, 143, 146, 153, 154, 160, 164
Chanctonbury Ring 65
Changi POW Camp 149, 188, 223
Charterhouse School 114
Chard, Somerset 93, 232
Charles IX of France 11
Chaucer Hospital, Canterbury 56
Chequers 64
Cherbourg [WW2] 179
Chichester 127
Christ Church, Oxford 55, 65, 68, 69, 175
Christ College, Finchley 16, 153, 158,
Church Lane, Lyminster 7, 22, 24, 53, 63, 160, 173, 200, 202
Churchill tanks 193
Churchill, Sir Winston 64, 86, 110, 143, 163-165, 177, 187, 196, 217
Clapton Flower Show 128
Clapton Primary School 229
Clovelly 132, 133
Clutsam, Mr. G. H. [West End Musical Producer] 92
Cohen, Barbara [American friend of Vi Brown and English Speaking Union] 229
Cold War 217
Coley family [Cooper relatives] 112
Collingwood Australian Rules Football and Cricket Club [Melbourne] 93
Combe St. Nicholas [Nr. Chard] 93, 232
Coates, Lt. Col. [Singapore Hospital, Japanese invasion] 186, 187
Combles [WW1] 32
3 Commando 139, 205, 218
4 Commando 205

5 Commando 206
6 Commando 205
43 Commando 204
45 Commando 205
46 Commando 218
Commonwealth Party 211
Compton, Denis 20
Cooden Beach Golf Club 46
Cooper, Atholl 13, 14, 35, 153, 224, 230
Cooper, Dr. Basil 10, 13, 14, 32, 153
Cooper, Brenda 9, 10, 14, 15, 36, 44, 122, 230
Cooper, Major Cecil 2,10, 12-15, 23, 25, 28-42, 44, 50, 55, 60, 61, 68, 109, 112, 119-122, 124, 132, 133, 136-139, 153, 156, 159-161, 167, 171, 178, 182, 183, 186, 199, 207-216,219-223, 227, 230-232
Cooper, Charles H 14, 186
Cooper, Dorothy [Dolly] 10, 14, 15, 183
Cooper, Elsie 10, 14, 15, 230
Cooper, George M.P. for Bermondsey 112
Cooper, Linda [nee' Metherall] 2, 31, 33, 35-42, 60, 80, 81, 93-95, 98, 109, 119-122, 124, 132, 133, 136-139, 153, 156, 159,-161, 167, 171, 178, 182, 183, 186, 199, 207-216, 219-223, 227, 230-232
Cooper, Margaret [wife of Richard] 9, 32, 128, 231, 232
Cooper, Margaret [sister of Charles Cecil] 12,15
Cooper, Maud 58, 80, 88, 91, 92, 100, 121, 142, 180, 181, 203, 211
Cooper, Polly 2, 17, 21, 22, 24, 34-36, 38-40, 51-53, 80, 88, 94-96, 98, 100, 119-122, 132, 133,145, 159, 166, 168, 171, 173, 182-184,212, 222, 226, 231, 232
Cooper, Richard 2, 9, 17, 21, 24, 36, 38, 39-41, 48, 51-53, 80, 81, 94, 96, 98, 101, 119-122, 120-123, 128, 133, 134, 159, 167,-169, 182, 184, 212, 222, 226, 231, 232
Cooper, Sally [nee' Court] 14
Cooper, Sydie 100

Corman, Margaret [American friend of Vi Brown and English Speaking Union] 229
Cornwall 132
Coward, Noel 72
Cowdrey, Lord 5
Cowper, William [Poet] 50, 53
Crabtree, Godfrey [Trifler] 113, 124
Craig, Dr. Donald 99
Craxton, Anthony [BBC] 19, 20, 56, 141
Craxton family 19, 20, 56
Crawford, Michael [actor] 99
Crewkerne, Somerset 4, 27, 32, 62, 109, 127-129, 180, 226, 228, 229, 232, 233, 235
Cricketer magazine 54, 55, 117, 144, 156
Croce de Guerra 153
Croix de Guerre 233
Croley, Mary 81, 82
Cromwell, Oliver 11
Cross, Edith [North London Collegiate School] 231
Cross of St. George of Russia 31, 34, 74
Countess of Burma 73
Croydon Airport [Munich Crisis]143
Curtis, Richard [Blackadder] 14
Czechoslovakian Crisis 123, 142, 145

D

D Day 4, 74, 139, 201-206, 209, 209, 218
Dad's Army 161
Dalton, Judy [nee' Tegart] 109
Dead End Canal [Battle of Ypres] 31
Delhi 72
Dieppe Raid 4, 186, 192-194
Dobie, Col. [Parachute Regiment at Arnhem] 210

Docherty, Richard "Only The Enemy in Front" [Every Other Bugger Behind] - The Recce Corps at War 1940-46" 203
Docklands 79-83
D'Olivera, Basil 57
Doll, Sir Richard 47, 48, 52, 55, 56, 107-109, 113, 124, 164
Doll, Christopher 109
Dorchester Hotel, London 70
Douglas, Josephine [BBC] 109
Dragons CC [Harpenden] 153, 155
Drogheda 11
Drummond, Matron [Singapore Massacre] 188
Drummond, Mrs. [Headmistress of The North London Collegiate School for Girls] 231
Drummondswood [Wayford nr. Crewkerne] 231
Duke family [Lyminster] 96, 97, 122
Duke's Field, Lyminster 97
Duke of Kent 173
Duke of Norfolk 21, 23
Duke of Norfolk's XI 158
Dunkirk 154, 164, 165, 168
Dunlop, C. R. [Scottish cricketer] 114
Durban Cricket Ground 115
Duval, Rev. 52, 53, 80, 94-96, 98, 121, 122, 161
Duval, Mrs. 80, 95, 121, 122

E

Eaton, J. A. [Trifler] 156, 157
Eden, Anthony [Government Minister and later Prime Minster] 143
Eaton, Jack [Sussex CCC] 116, 117
Edgar, Robin [Triflers' CC] 75, 83, 85, 117
Edinburgh Academicals CC 113, 141, 142, 148, 149

Edinburgh Academy 88, 113, 140, 199, 211
Eindhoven [WW2] 213
Elgar, Edward 1, 7
Elizabeth R [BBC Series] 22
Elizabethan, The [Westminster School magazine] 69, 105
Elkington, Capt. [Royal Welch Fusiliers] 189, 190
Elson, J 116
Elton, Ben 14
Emmanual School, London 229
Emmott, Evelyn [Amberley Castle] 26, 169, 170
Endersby, Harold [Lyminster] 99, 100, 139, 185, 200, 232
Engleheart, Jock [Triflers' CC] 53
English Speaking Union 197
English Ladies Golf Championships 46
ENSA 213
Epsom College 68, 145, 146
Equal Opportunities Commission 3
Essendon Airport, Melbourne 224
Essex CCC 74, 115
Eteville [Battle of Normandy] 203
Evers, Dick [Fettes College & Triflers' CC] 112, 118, 150, 156, 157

F

Fabian Society 26, 44, 195
Fairey Swordfish aircraft 173
Fairey Albecore aircraft 173
Falaise Pocket [Battle of Normandy] 206
Federation of Understy Women 229
Felpham, West Sussex 107, 179
Ferguson, Pilot Officer [ADC to the Duke of Kent] 173, 174
Fergusson, Mrs. [Lyminster] 96, 180
Fettes College, Edinburgh 112

Finchley 12, 14, 15, 16, 28, 29, 47, 112, 122, 132, 153, 161, 185
Flanders 29-31
Fletcher's XI, P. C. 114
Flood, Brigadier G.R. 99, 124, 130, 215
Flood family 99, 124, 130, 168, 182, 232
Flood, John 130, 168, 182, 232
Flood, Yeoma 99, 168, 182
Foot, Rt. Hon. Michael 154, 164
Ford, RNAS / RAF base 20, 26, 150, 162, 170-174, 179, 191, 195, 200
Foreman, John [Author of "The Battle of Britain : The Forgotten Months"] 179
Foster, J. H. [cricketer] 117
Franco-Prussian War 58
Frost, Lt. Col. John [Parachute Regiment] 210
Fry, Stephen [comedian] 14

G

Gale, Maj. Gen. "Windy" 106, 107, 205, 206
Gallipoli 5
Gaparb [WW1] 29
Garbo [WW2 spy] 176
Gargoyles C. C. 128
Gasteen, Mr. [nouveau riche owner of Lyminster House in the 60s] 233, 234
Gawthorne, Paddy [Triflers' C. C.] 156-158
General Election of 1950 127
General de Gaulle 64, 209
General Strike 25, 49
Gennap, Holland [Liberation of] 214, 215
Georgia, U. S. A. 197
Germany 61, 62, 86-88, 108-112, 123, 131, 142, 143, 146, 160, 161, 166, 174, 175, 196, 206, 207, 215-220

Gibbon, Muriel [Girton College, Cambridge] 15
Gibraltar 165
Gilbert, Sir Martin [historian] 73
Gilligan family [cricket] 74, 75, 105
Girton College, Cambridge 8, 15, 26, 46, 135, 170, 195
Glasgow 199
Glindinning, Sgt. J. N. [RAF] 179
Gloucester 142
Gloucestershire CCC 67
Gower, David 57
Godalming CC 137, 138
Goering, Hermann 6, 172
Gonet, Edmund [Triflers' CC] 141
Goodwood Golf Club [Sussex] 202
Grace, W. G. 16
Graham, David [1933 Oxford Union "King and Country" Debate] 70
Grainger Prize 104
Grant, Dr. Ronald 166, 167
Grant, Nancy 166, 167
Grave Bridge [Arnhem] 213
Great Britain Olympic athletics squad 8, 111
Greig, Tony [Captain of the England Cricket team] 136
Griffith, S. C. "Billy" [Sec. of the MCC] 105, 106, 144, 205
Guernsey cattle 17, 24, 42, 62, 184, 200, 227, 228, 231-233

H

Halifax, Lord 164-166
Hampshire CCC 67, 204
Hampton Court fire [1987] 107
Harlequins CC 175
Hill 60, Ypres 75

Hanover [WW2] 28, 207, 216, 219, 220
Hannoversche Allgemeine [newspaper] 207, 216, 219
Harpenden 153
Hattingen POW Camp 219
Havant CC 16, 65-67, 84, 85, 107
Heard, Eric [Nephew of Cardinal Heard & Triflers' CC] 124, 129, 156
Hearn, Avis [WAAF, Poling Radar Station] 172
Heaton, Neville [Triflers' CC & 1944 Education Act] 126
Heffer, Simon [journalist] 57
Hicks, David 73
Hicks, Lady Pamela 73
Highland Division [WW2] 179
Hilder's XI, A. F. 145
Hindenburg, President 62
Hitler, Adolf 1, 7, 8, 61, 62, 70, 71, 86-88, 110, 111, 123, 131, 136, 137, 142, 143, 146, 154, 157, 164, 165, 174, 178, 221
Hitlerjugand Panzers [12th] 206
Hoare, Sir Samuel [Chamberlain Government] 146
Hobbs, Sir Jack [Surrey CCC and England] 3, 115
Holden, C. J. "Juggy" [Captain of Steyning CC] 65, 85
Holohan, Sgt. Maj. [Royal Regiment of Canada at the Dieppe Raid] 191-193
Holland 207, 209-215, 221
Holmes, Aubrey [Husband of Elsie Cooper] 14
Holmes, Dorothy [Australian relative]14, 230
Holyrood Palace 12
Hong Kong 185
Hoole family [Lyminster] 80
Horsham 45
House of Commons Cricket XI 153
Howard, Peter ["Guilty Men"] 154
Huguenots 11
Humanism 161

Hutchison, Stephen [Loretto School CC & Triflers' CC] 112
Hurricanes 171, 174
Hussars 7th [WW1] 28
Hussars 19th [WW1] 28, 29
Hutton, Sir Leonard 137
Huxley, Aldous 72

I

India 46, 71-73, 95, 99, 101, 139
Institute of Advanced Motorists 64
Ireland, M. N. [Bognor Regis CC] 75
Irish Rugby Football Union 146
Isle of Dogs 21, 26, 79, 81
Isle of Wight [WW2] 173

J

Jacobites 138
Jardine, Douglas [Captain of the MCC on the 1933 Bodyline Tour] 132, 135
Japanese Army 186-188
Jarrow March 108
Jelly, Victor [Lyminster] 200
Jessop, Gilbert [England cricketer] 16, 67
Jessop, Rev. G. L. O. 16, 67, 85
Jewish persecution in Austria 166
Joad, C. E. M. [1933 Oxford Union Debate] 70, 71
Johnson, Brian [BBC Test Match Special] 20
Johnson, Johnnie [Slinfold CC] 125, 150, 151
Jones, Iris ["Littlehampton at War"] 161
Jordan, Mr. [High Commissioner for New Zealand] 194

K

Kaiser 29
Kamp Lintfort [Germany, WW2] 218
Kashmir 73
Kansas 197
Kenley [RAF] 147
Kent CCC 5
Kentucky 197
Kenyan Kongonis CC 157
Krefield [Germany WW2] 218
Kilner, Mary 49
Kimberley, Mr. [Docklands "self-help" project, 1930s] 79-81
King Alfred, [HMS] 194
King, Mrs. [Lyminster] 96
King's College Hospital 102
Kingswood School, Bath 9, 47, 48, 111, 112, 184, 199, 208, 222
Kinloch, A [Trifler] 113
Kinsella, Matron [Fall of Singapore and Japanese atrocities] 188
Kitchener, Lord 2, 28, 207, 209
Klein Zillebeke [WW1] 29
Knight, Donald [Surrey CCC, England and Triflers' CC] 114, 115
Knucker Hole [Lyminster] 95, 96
Kotze [1904 South African Cricket team] 16

L

LAA Battery [38th], Canadian Army 194
Labour Party 25, 49, 127
La Gorgue, Flanders [1572 St. Bartholomew's Day Massacre] 11
Lake Doiran [WW1] 122

Lancaster, Doris [Wife of Canadian soldier WW2] 194
Lancing College, Sussex 130
Land Girls 135, 195
Lane, Bob [Lyminster] 97, 98, 101
Langley family [Manangatang, Australia] 34
Langridge, John [Sussex C. C. C.] 67
Lansdown Hill, Bath 199
Larwood, Harold [England cricketer] 135
Latey, Sir John [High Court judge] 52, 55, 64, 65
Launceston, Cornwall 132
Law, Jack "Commandos and Rangers of World War Two" 218
League of Nations 110, 143
Leese [V2 rocket site in Germany] 218
Le Mans [WW2] 206
Le Plein [Normandy Campaign] 206
Lee, Elizabeth [nee' Metherall] 109
Ley [German Armaments Minister] 43
Lepine family [Huguenot Cooper ancestors] 12
Lespine, Jehan de [Huguenot refugee] 11
Lewsdon Hill, Dorset 228
"Lilac Time" [musical] 92
Limpley Stoke [nr. Bath] 14, 183
Lillee, Dennis [Australian cricketer] 135
Littlehampton 21, 24, 58, 59, 81, 99, 134, 168, 174, 184, 193
Littlehampton CC 15, 19, 47, 59, 63, 148, 171, 174
Lloyd George, David 72
Lloyds of London 14, 19
Lockwood [Steyning CC fast bowler] 66
Lohning, General [Commandant, Ahlem Concentration Camp, nr, Hanover] 219
Lomas, J. M. [Oxford University CC] 204
London University 153
Lonsdale, Maj. Gen. Erroll [Triflers' C. C.] 52, 55, 64

Lords Cricket Ground 16, 19, 20, 67, 204
Loretto School 112-114, 140, 148
Lovatt, Brigadier Lord 205
Luftwaffe 7, 165, 171-174
Lyminster 1, 2, 4, 6, 7, 17, 19-27, 36, 37, 39-43, 45, 48, 50, 52, 54, 55, 58, 59, 61, 63, 67, 69, 74, 77-80, 82, 87, 90, 92, 95-97, 100, 103, 108, 116-122, 124, 128-130, 135, 138, 139, 142, 145-147, 149-153, 156-163, 166-169, 172, 174, 178, 179, 182, 184, 185, 188-196,199, 200, 202, 203, 211, 212, 214, 218, 223, 224, 227, 233- 235
Lyminster Church, Sussex 22, 95, 97, 162, 163
Lyminster Cup, Clapton Flower Show, nr. Crewkerne 128, 229
Lyminster Farm, Crewkerne 4, 16, 17, 62, 122, 167, 231, 232, 236
Lyminster Farm, Sussex 17, 94, 184
Lyminster House, Sussex 1, 2, 4, 6, 19-27, 36, 37, 43, 45, 51-54, 58, 69, 79, 80-82, 90-92, 97-99, 116, 117, 119-122, 124, 138, 142, 150, 156, 167-169, 174, 178, 182, 184, 191, 192, 195, 200, 202, 203, 211, 223, 224, 233, 234
Lyminster House CC, Sussex 21, 36, 53, 55, 79, 82, 100, 101, 137, 139
Lyminster House Tea Dances during WW2 92, 162, 179, 191-195
Lynmouth 132
Lynton 132
Lyric Theatre, Shaftesbury Avenue 92

M

Maas, River 210
MacDonald J. A. [Triflers' CC & Lyminster House CC] 124, 126, 137, 139
Machrie Golf Course[Isle of Islay] 46
MacPherson, A. J. S. [Edinburgh Academicals CC] 149

Madagascar 139
Mair, C. J. R. [Scottish cricketer] 114

Major, Rt. Hon. John 57
Malin, Sarah [Actress and grand daughter of John Alderson] 139
Mallee [Northern Victoria] 34, 35, 40, 41, 60
Malta [WW2] 165
Manangatang, Victoria, Australia 24, 33, 34, 39, 60, 136
Marne, Battle of the 29, 136
Manderston CC 113, 114, 140, 148
March into the Rhineland, 1936 110
Masterman, Sir John [XXX Committee WW2] 55, 69, 70, 71, 77, 175-177
Mathews, J. K. [Worting CC and Sussex CCC] 144, 158
Mathews, Miss [Federation of University Women] 229
Mauchlan, Percy [Royal Engineers] 180
McCabe, Stan [1938 Australian team] 136
MCC 5, 16, 57, 85, 103, 106, 107, 135, 177
McIvor, Colin [Ashtead CC & Harlequins CC] 175
"Mein Kampf" 221
Meise, Uff 3 [German pilot] 179
Melbourne 12, 38, 93, 131
Melbourne Cricket Ground 93
Melbourne University 12
Menin Gate 74
Merville Battery [D Day] 205, 206
Messines [WW1] 29
Metherall family 12, 39, 109, 131, 132, 146, 167, 185, 191, 192
Metherall, Pilot Officer Jeff [Australian RAF] 182, 184, 188, 189
Methodism 1, 15, 32, 43, 47, 49, 92, 111, 121, 133, 161, 167
Meyer, Kurt [12th Hitlerjugand Panzers] 204

Middlesex Nomads CC 128
Middle Wallop [RAF] 172
Military Tournament 79
Miller, Glenn [Band Leader] 26, 179
Mills, Bob {Lyminster] 100, 184
Millwall 26, 27, 78, 79
Milman, Dermot [Triflers' CC & England rugby international] 143-146
Minister of Transport 13
Mitchener, Philip [Surgeon] 104
Modern Pentathlon Association 64
Moffat Golf Course 202
Moffat Hills 142
Mohawk [HMS] 97
Molotov-Von Ribbontrop Pact 157
Monkton Combe School, Bath 47
Mons, Battle of 136
Montgomery, General 206, 209
Monts de Cats [WW1] 29
Moreton Bay SS 38, 40
Morgan, Cliff [BBC & Welsh Rugby International] 111
Morgan, Maj. [Allied Control Commission] 214, 215
Morrisey, Shelagh [Lyminster Land Girl] 195
Morrison, Herbert 143, 164
Mosley family 22, 233, 234
Mosley, Nicolas [Lord Ravensdale] 22, 233
Mosley, Sir Oswald 22, 233
Mosquito aircraft 17, 191, 200
Mosquito crash on the Lyminster House cricket ground 200
Mould, E. A. F. [Steyning C. C. scorer] 66
Mountbatten, Lord 51, 68, 72, 73
Mulberry Harbours [D Day] 208
Munich Crisis 1938 142, 143
Munich Olympics 1972 64

Munro, Ian [Triflers' CC] 55
Murray River, Australia 41
Murray, Sgt. [236 Royal Engineers WW2] 179
Mussleborough 113
Mussolini, Benito 88, 147, 165

N

National Liberals 153
Nazi Party 61, 62, 71, 87, 88, 108, 110, 119, 123, 131, 147, 164, 166, 176, 216
Nazi War Criminals 164
Nelson's XI, R. P. 145
Neuve Chapelle [WW1] 31
Newnham College, Cambridge 15
New York 190
New Zealand 74, 194, 195
Nichols, Beverly [Writer] 69
Nijmegan [Arnhem Campaign] 210
Norfolk Arms, Steyning 60, 65
Normandy Campaign 202-207
North African Campaign 196
North London Collegiate School for Girls 14, 15, 46, 231
North Perrott CC 46, 94
Northern Victoria 24, 27, 32-41, 60, 136
Norway 37
Norwegian Campaign 167
Nottingham 136, 141
Nuremberg 71
Nuremberg Laws 88
Nuremberg Trials 164
"Nyarrin", Lyminster 24, 122, 159, 171
Nyarrin [village in Northern Victoria] 24
Nyarrin, Wayford, nr. Crewkerne 226

O

Oakes, C [Sussex CCC] 117
Oakes, J [Sussex CCC] 117, 144
Old Brightonians CC 55
Old Carthusians CC 114
Old Contemptibles, World War One 208
Old Dovonians CC 157
Old Westminsters CC 55, 56
Omaha Beach [D Day] 206
Oosterbeck War Cemetery 211
Operation "Market Garden" 209-211
Ormel, Mt [Normandy Campaign] 206
Osborne, Mr. [Butler, Lyminster House] 92, 93, 121
Osborne, Mrs. Connie [Maid, Lyminster House] 92, 93, 121
Osnabruck, Germany 218
Otterburn, Percy Arms 141
Oval Cricket Ground 136
Oxfordshire CCC 177
Oxford Union Debate, 1933 ["For King and Country"] 70
Oxford University 70, 74, 115, 145, 176, 202, 204
Ouistream [D Day] 205
Owen, Frank ["Guilty Men"] 154
Owens, Jesse [1936 Berlin Olympics] 111, 178

P

Pakistan 73
Palairet, L [Somerset CCC and England] 3
Parachute Regiment 130, 209, 210, 215
Parker, J. B. [Havant CC & Hampshire CCC] 85
Parkman, Tom [North Perrott CC] 46

Pagan, Francis [Founder member of the Triflers' XI] 52, 55, 58, 63, 65, 68, 69, 75, 85, 105, 108, 113, 114, 115, 117, 118, 138, 143-145, 156, 157, 174
Pas de Calais [WW2] 176
Pasche, Matron [Fall of Singapore and Japanese atrocities] 188
Paulus, Field Marshall 196
Payne, Miss J. J. [Old Girtonian] 170
Paynter, Eddie [Lancashire CC & England] 136
Peacock Scholarship 104
Pearce, G [Sussex CCC] 116, 117
Peebles, Scotland 113, 114
Pegasus Bridge [D Day] 205
Percival, Gen. [Invasion of Singapore] 187
Percival Proctor aircraft 173
Persia 139
Perthshire 9
Pettingill, Dr. [American Professor of Economics] 229
Philby, Kim [spy] 68, 69
Philippines [WW2] 197
Pilsden Pen, Dorset 227, 228
Poland 7, 143, 165, 171
Poland, German invasion of 7
Poling 20, 26
Poling Radar Station 26, 162, 170-173, 179
Polish Army 206
Pompeii 118
Porlock, Somerset 49
Port Melbourne 38, 131, 224
Port Said, Egypt 40
Price, Alfred "The Hardest Day" 172
Prince Max of Hesse [WW1] 29
Prince of Wales, HMS 186
Promenade Concerts 59
Proud, R. B. [Oxford University CC] 204

Psyche [Cooper family dog] 232
"Punch" 28

Q

Quaker religion 26, 230
Queenie Nurcombe [Lyminster] 184
Queen's Christmas Message 56
Quiltor, David [actor] 73
Quislings [Dutch collaborators with the Nazis] 212

R

Radley College 102
Raeburn Place, Edinburgh 113
Ranji [England Cricket team] 3
Ravensdale, Lord [Nicolas Mosley] 22, 233
Rea, Hon. Findlay [Triflers' CC & The Cricketer magazine] 126, 155, 157
"Reach for the Sky" 17
Reading University 15, 130
Refreshers CC 128, 149
Reichstag 62, 71
Reninghelst [WW1] 31
Repulse, HMS 186
Rheinberg War Cemetery 219
Rhine, Crossing of 4, 139, 206, 217
Rhineland 110, 123
Rhodes, Jonty 54
Rice, Bill [Lyminster Court] 233
Rich, Jack [BBC and Triflers' CC] 52, 55, 113, 124, 141, 156, 158
Rijn, River [Holland] 210
RMS Grampion 33
Robertson, Jack [England cricket team] 106

Rommel, Field Marshall 207
Rooseveldt's New Deal 298
Rosedean School, Lampeter 184
"Rosemary for Remembrance" [Rosemary Sisson] 235
Rowntree family 26
Royal Army Service Corps 64, 226
Royal Artillery CC 175
Royal Ballet 88
Royal Chest Hospital, London 102
Royal College of Physicians 109
Royal College of Surgeons 66, 105
Royal Engineers 28, 179, 212
Royal Engineers CC 175
Royal Horse Artillery [WW1] 29
Royal Horse Guards [The Blues] 16
Royal East Kents "The Buffs" 31, 222
Royal Marines CC 18
Royal Observer Corps 23
Royal Regiment of Canada 191-194
Royal Welch Fusiliers 189, 190
Russell, Jack [Essex CCC & England] 115, 116
Russian looting in Germany 220
Russian POW's 216
Rustington [West Sussex] 24, 168, 173
Ryes War Cemetery, Normandy 203

S

Saladin 11
Salisbury 71
Salmon, Air Chief Marshall Sir William Geoffrey 22, 233
Salmon, Rosemary [wife of Nicolas Mosley, Lord Ravensdale] 22, 233
Salonica 32, 122, 222
Sandringham 56, 121

Sandhurst 130
Scottish Rugby XV 114, 146, 202
Scott family [Cooper relations] 112
Scottish Wayfarers CC 113, 140, 148
Seaforth Highlanders 139, 205
Sea Lake, Northern Victoria 35
Seelhurst atrocity carried out by the SS 220, 221
Sicily 118, 196
St. Bartholomew's Hospital, London 14, 32
St. George's Hospital, London 141
St. George's School, Harpenden 153
St. James Church, Piccadilly 73
St. John's School, Leatherhead 146
St. John's Wood 19, 37, 93, 141
St. Luke's Hospital, Chelsea 103, 104
St. Petersburg 62
St. Thomas Hospital, London 55, 104, 108
Scotland 9, 49, 50, 58, 110, 112-114, 140, 141, 148, 149
Selincourt, Hugh de [writer and cricketer] 50, 75, 76
Serengoon grass [Used in preparation of vitamin drinks at Changi] 188

Shaw, Pilot Officer [Australian RAF] 188, 189
Sherborne, Dorset 180, 231
Sherborne School, Dorset 90
Shiel, C. M. R. [Scottish cricketer] 114
Siberia 217
Sinclair, Archibald [Liberal Party] 72
Singapore Hospital 186, 187
Singapore [fall of] 4, 186-188
Six Wives of Henry 8th [BBC series] 22
Slater, Lt. [Canadian Black Watch] 180, 181
Smiley, Capt, Thomas [RAMC] 187
Sisson family [Lyminster] 22, 101, 162

Sisson, Rosemary Anne 22, 101, 162, 168, 178, 179, 233, 235
Six Bells, Lyminster 101, 191
Slimbridge Wildlife Trust 68
Slinfold CC 123, 125, 126, 149-151
Smith of Marlow, Lord [Triflers' CC & Surgeon] 65, 66, 104, 105, 124
Sobers, Sir Garfield 93
Socialism 27
"Some Mother's do Have 'em" [BBC comedy] 99
Somerset CCC 3, 17
Somerset Cricket League 6
Somme, Battle of 32, 183
South African Cricket team 16, 107, 115
South African Rugby XV 146
Southampton 28, 40
South Herts Golf Club 46
Spanish Civil War 109
Special Service Brigade [D Day] 205
Spencer, Frank [actor] 99
Spitfire aircraft 17, 109, 171
SS Panzers [9th] 210
SS Vyner Brook 188
Stalin, Josef 147, 164
Stallibrass, J [Bognor Regis CC & Triflers' CC] 157, 158
Stanford family [Slinfold CC] 123, 125, 126
Stanley Military Hospital, Hong Kong 185
Steer, Trevor [Collingwood Australian Rules team] 93
Sterling bombers 191
Steyning CC 65-67, 78, 85, 137, 149
Stocker, Sir John [Triflers' CC & High Court Judge] 56, 129-131
Storrington CC 50, 67, 75-77, 147
Stuka aircraft 171-174
Sudetenland 123, 142, 143

Suez Canal 40
Suffolk CCC 63
Surrey CCC 104, 115
Sussex CCC 45, 46, 67, 105-107, 112, 116, 117, 144, 145
"Sussex Life" 69
Sussex Martlets CC 55, 67, 116, 157
Swanton, E. W. [Daily Telegraph] 55-58
Sword Beach [D Day] 139, 205
Symes-Thompson, Edmund 102-104, 124, 141, 142, 144
Sydney Hill [Sydney Cricket Ground] 136

T

Tai Tam Peninsular [WW2] 185
Tangmere [RAF] 17, 162, 171, 179, 191, 195
Taormina 118
Taylor, Claude [Oxford University & Leicestershire CCC] 114, 115
Tennesee Valley Project 198
"Test Match Special" 20
Thompson, Capt. B. J. [Royal Engineers] 179
Thompson, Capt. [Royal Regiment of Canada] 191, 193
Thompson, Jeff [Australian cricketer] 13
Thorburn, W. B. [Triflers' CC] 113, 156
Tite Scholarship 104
Tod, B. R. [Scottish cricketer] 114
Tod, R [Scottish cricketer] 114
Toddington Cemetery, West Sussex 174
Tomsett, Tom [Lyminster] 101
Toronto 193
Torgau [Allied armies meet at] 217
Town family [Lyminster] 97
Trent Bridge Cricket Ground 141
Triflers' CC 4, 7, 17, 21, 25, 48, 50-56, 58-59, 63-69, 71, 73-78, 83-85, 87-88, 90, 102-108, 112-118, 124-131, 137,

139-144, 148-151, 155-160,, 163, 166, 169, 174, 175, 181, 191, 204, 205, 209, 229
Trinity College, Cambridge 55, 68-9, 88
Trueleigh Radar Station 173
Turkish Cavalry [WW1] 122
Turner, J. F. [Triflers' CC] 113, 139
Twickenham 16
Typhoon aircraft 191

U

Uppingham School 145, 184, 199
"Upstairs Downstairs" [TV Series] 22
Urquhart, Gen. [Arnhem] 210
Utah Beach [D Day] 206
Utrecht [WW2] 212

V

Vardon, Harry [English golfer and Open Championship winner] 46
Vaughan-Thomas, Wynford [BBC] 217
VE Day 214, 221, 222, 224
Vermont, USA 197
Versailles Treaty 61, 70, 88, 101, 131, 168
Virginia, USA 112, 196
Vlamerthinghe [WW1] 31
Vlijmen [Holland] 213
Voce, Bill [1933 Bodyline MCC Tour to Australia] 135
Von Kluge, Gen. [German Army] 207

W

Waal river [Arnhem] 210
Wadham School, Crewkerne 94

Wagingen [WW2] 211
Wagner 6
Walker, Cpl. [Royal Engineers] 180
Wallace, Nellie [Music hall] 81
Walrus Seaplane 195
Wanganui Grammar School, New Zealand 74
Warwick School 111
Wayford, Nr. Crewkerne 27, 109, 127, 180, 228-231
Wayford Manor Farm, Nr. Crewkerne 213, 226-231
Weimar Republic 61
Weir D. [Scottish cricketer] 114
Welsh Rugby XV 146
Wesley, John 40
Wells, Geoffrey [Lyminster] 161
Wessex Division [43rd] 203
Westminster Ramblers CC 128, 129
Westminster School 4, 19, 21, 25, 37, 50, 52-55, 68-69, 105, 115, 128, 138
West, Peter [BBC] 20
West Point, USA 197
Wexford 11
Whitelaw, Freddie "Thunderbum" [Triflers' CC] 112, 117, 124, 142
Wilhemina Canal 210
Willems Canal [WW2] 210
Williams, Sir Max Harries 99
Wimbledon tennis 109
Woolminstone, Nr. Crewkerne 122, 231, 232
Woodruff, Frank 13, 89, 153
Woodruff, Prof. Harold 10, 12, 37-38, 224
Woodruff, Philip 12, 30, 37, 38, 229
Woodruff, Prof. Sir Michael 12, 37, 38, 149, 186-188, 223, 229
Woodruff, Tony 99
Woodruff, Mary 99

Woodruff, Steph 99
Woolley, Frank [Kent CCC & England] 107
Wootton Bassett 142
Worcester College, Oxford 70
Worcester Royal Grammar School 111
Wormwood Scrubs prison 80
Worthing CC 67, 144-146, 159
Wright, Prof. R.D. 223

X

XVth Scottish Division XV 202

Y

Yamoshita, Comm. [Japanese War Criminal] 187, 188
Yapton 46
Yorkshire Education Committee 111
Ypres [WW1] 3, 29-31, 74
Young, Maj. Peter ["Storm from the Sea"] 205
Yugoslavia 207

Z

Zenana Mission 95
Zena's Laddie 42